Mandalay National Wildlife Refuge

Comprehensive Conservation Plan

U.S. Department of the Interior
Fish and Wildlife Service
Southeast Region

October 2009

Submitted by: _Paul Yakupzack_   Date: _8-5-09_
Paul Yakupzack, Refuge Manager
Mandalay NWR

Concur: _Ken Litzenberger_   Date: _8-9-09_
Ken Litzenberger, Project Leader
Southeast Louisiana Refuges Complex

Concur: _____   Date: _8-17-09_
for Ricky Ingram, Refuge Supervisor
Southeast Region

Concur: _____   Date: _9/11/09_
for Jon Andrew, Regional Chief
Southeast Region

Approved by: _____   Date: _9/14/9_
for Sam Hamilton, Regional Director
(Acting) Southeast Region

COMPREHENSIVE CONSERVATION PLAN

MANDALAY NATIONAL WILDLIFE REFUGE

Terrebonne Parish, Louisiana

U.S. Department of the Interior
Fish and Wildlife Service

Southeast Region
Atlanta, Georgia

September 2009

TABLE OF CONTENTS

COMPREHENSIVE CONSERVATION PLAN

LIST OF FIGURES

LIST OF TABLES

Executive Summary

The Fish and Wildlife Service (Service) has prepared this Comprehensive Conservation Plan (CCP) to guide the management of Mandalay National Wildlife Refuge (NWR) in Terrebonne Parish, Louisiana. The CCP outlines programs and corresponding resource needs for the next 15 years, as mandated by the National Wildlife Refuge System Improvement Act of 1997.

Before the Service began planning, it conducted a biological review of the refuge's wildlife and habitat management program and conducted public scoping meetings to solicit public opinion of the issues the plan should address. The biological review team was composed of biologists from federal and state agencies and non-governmental organizations that have an interest in the refuge. The refuge staff held one public scoping meeting. Also, a 30-day public review and comment period of the draft comprehensive conservation plan and environmental assessment was provided.

The Service developed and analyzed three alternatives. Alternative A was a proposal to maintain the status quo. Under this alternative, no new actions would be taken to improve or enhance the refuge's current habitat, wildlife, and public use management programs. The existing programs would be continued with no changes. Species of federal responsibility, such as threatened and endangered species and migratory birds, would continue to be monitored at present levels. Additional species monitoring would occur as opportunistic events when contacts or volunteers offer support. Current programs of marsh management would be maintained with no improvements or adaptations. No progressive wetland restoration projects would be implemented. All public use programs of fishing, hunting, wildlife observation, wildlife photography, and environmental education and interpretation would continue at present levels and with current facilities. No programs or facilities would be updated or expanded.

Acquisition of lands into the refuge would occur when funding is appropriated and willing sellers offer land that is quality waterfowl habitat. Staff would consist of a manager and a biologist supporting both Mandalay and Bayou Teche NWRs, along with supplementary support from the remainder of the Southeast Louisiana NWR Complex staff when needed. The refuge headquarters would serve only as administrative offices with no enhancement of the grounds for public use and interpretation.

Alternative B proposed management of the natural resources of Mandalay NWR based on maintaining and improving wetland habitats, monitoring targeted flora and fauna representative of the Terrebonne Basin, and providing quality public use programs and wildlife-dependent recreational activities. All species occurring on the refuge would be considered and certain targeted species would be managed for and monitored in addition to species of federal responsibility. These species would be chosen based on the criteria that they are indicators of the health of important habitat or species of concern.

Wetland loss would be documented and, whenever possible, restored. Public use programs would be improved by offering more facilities and wildlife observation areas. Public use facilities would undergo annual reviews for maintenance needs and safety concerns. Overall public use would be monitored to determine if any negative impacts would occur to refuge resources from overuse. Education programs would be reviewed and improved to complement current refuge management and current staffing. Archaeological resources would be surveyed.

Land acquisitions within the approved acquisition boundary would be based on importance of the habitat for target management species. The refuge headquarters would not only house small administrative offices, but offer interpretation of refuge wildlife and habitats, as well as demonstrate habitat improvements for individual landowners. The main interpretive facilities would be housed at the Southeast Louisiana NWR Complex in Lacombe, Louisiana.

In general, under Alternative B, management decisions and actions would support wildlife species and habitat occurring on the refuge based on well-planned strategies and sound scientific judgment. Quality wildlife-dependent recreational uses, environmental education, and interpretation programs would be offered to support and explain the natural resources of the refuge.

Alternative C proposed managing the natural resources of Mandalay NWR for maximized public use activities including wildlife-dependent recreational activities. The majority of staff time and efforts would support public use activities including hunting, fishing, wildlife observation, wildlife photography, and environmental education and interpretation. Federal trust species and archaeological resources would be monitored as mandated, but other species targeted for management would depend on which ones the public is interested in utilizing.

All refuge programs for conservation of wildlife and habitat, such as monitoring, surveying, and managing marsh, would support species and resources of importance for public use. Emphasis would be placed more on interpreting and demonstrating these programs than actual implementation. Providing access with trails and by dredging for boat access would be maximized, as well as providing public use facilities throughout the refuge.

Land acquisitions within the approved acquisition boundary would be based on importance of the habitat for public use. The refuge headquarters area would provide small administrative offices, a visitor center, and be developed for public use activities such as interpretation and outreach.

In general, under Alternative C, the focus of refuge management would be on expanding public use activities to the fullest extent possible while conducting only mandated resource protection such as conservation of threatened and endangered species, migratory birds, and archaeological resources.

Based on the mission of the National Wildlife Refuge System, the purposes for which Mandalay NWR was established, and the focus of the Lower Mississippi River Ecosystem priorities, the Service selected Alternative B, Resource-Focused Management, as the preferred management direction.

Implementing the preferred alternative will result in a diversity of habitats for a variety of fish and wildlife species, enhance resident wildlife populations, restore wetlands, and provide opportunities for a variety of compatible wildlife-dependent recreation, education, and interpretive activities.

I. Background

INTRODUCTION

This Comprehensive Conservation Plan (CCP) for Mandalay National Wildlife Refuge (NWR) was prepared to guide management actions and direction of the refuge. Fish and wildlife conservation will receive first priority in refuge management; wildlife-dependent recreation will be allowed and encouraged as long as it is compatible with, and does not detract from, the mission of the refuge or the purposes for which it was established.

A planning team developed a range of alternatives that best met the goals and objectives of the refuge and that could be implemented within the 15-year planning period. The draft of this CCP was made available to state and federal government agencies, non-governmental agencies, conservation partners, and the general public for review and comment. The comments from each entity were considered in the development of this CCP.

PURPOSE AND NEED FOR THE PLAN

The purpose of the CCP is to identify the role that Mandalay NWR will play in support of the mission of the National Wildlife Refuge System (Refuge System), and to provide long-term guidance to the refuge's management programs and activities for the next 15 years.

The CCP will:

- Provide a clear statement of the desired future conditions when refuge purposes and goals are accomplished;
- Provide refuge neighbors, visitors, and government officials with an understanding of Service management actions on and around the refuges;
- Ensure that Service management actions, including land protection and recreation/education programs, are consistent with the mandates of the Refuge System; and
- Provide a basis for the development of budget requests for operations, maintenance, and capital improvement needs.

FISH AND WILDLIFE SERVICE

The Service traces its roots to 1871, with the establishment of the Commission of Fisheries involved with research and fish culture. The once independent commission was renamed the Bureau of Fisheries and placed under the Department of Commerce and Labor in 1903.

The Service also traces its roots to 1886, with the establishment of a Division of Economic Ornithology and Mammalogy in the Department of Agriculture. In 1896, with a shift from research pertaining to the relationship of birds and animals to agriculture to the delineation of the range of plants and animals, the name was changed to the Division of Biological Survey.

On June 30, 1940, the Department of Commerce, Bureau of Fisheries, was combined with the Department of Agriculture, Bureau of Biological Survey, and transferred to the Department of the Interior as the Fish and Wildlife Service. The name was changed to the Bureau of Sport Fisheries and Wildlife in 1956 and finally to the Fish and Wildlife Service in 1974.

Figure 1. Location of Mandalay National Wildlife Refuge within the Southeast Louisiana
National Wildlife Refuge Complex

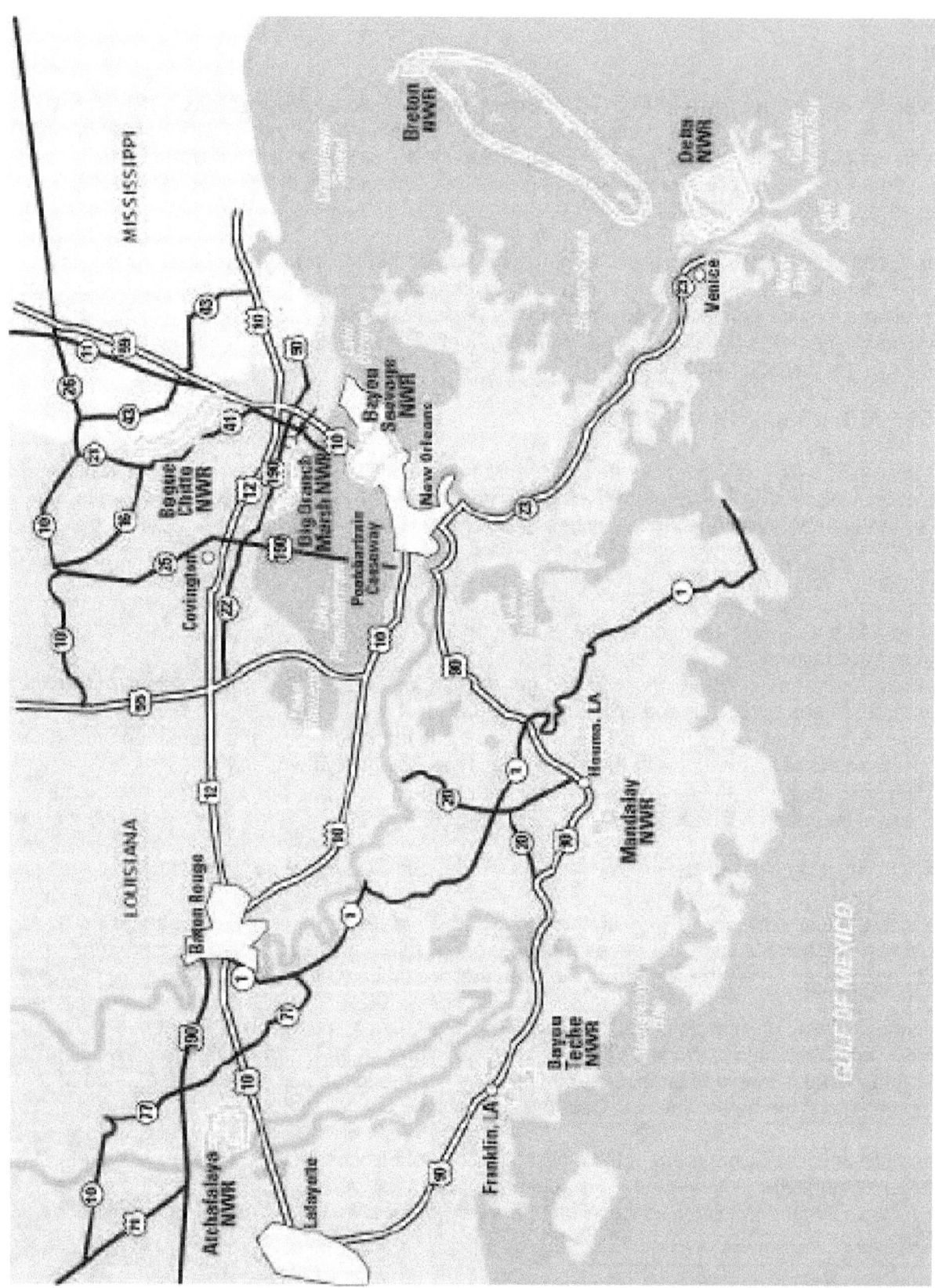

The Service, working with others, is responsible for conserving, protecting, and enhancing fish and wildlife and their habitats for the continuing benefit of the American people through federal programs relating to migratory birds, endangered species, interjurisdictional fish and marine mammals, and inland sport fisheries (142 DM 1.1).

As part of its mission, the Service manages more than 540 national wildlife refuges covering over 95 million acres. These areas comprise the National Wildlife Refuge System, the world's largest collection of lands set aside specifically for fish and wildlife. The majority of these lands, 77 million acres, is in Alaska. The remaining acres are spread across the other 49 states and several United States territories. In addition to refuges, the Service manages thousands of small wetlands, national fish hatcheries, 64 fishery resource offices, and 78 ecological services field stations. The Service enforces federal wildlife laws, administers the Endangered Species Act, manages migratory bird populations, restores nationally significant fisheries, conserves and restores wildlife habitat, and helps foreign governments with their conservation efforts. It also oversees the Federal Aid program that distributes hundreds of millions of dollars in excise taxes on fishing and hunting equipment to state fish and wildlife agencies.

NATIONAL WILDLIFE REFUGE SYSTEM

The mission of the National Wildlife Refuge System (Refuge System), as defined by the National Wildlife Refuge System Improvement Act of 1997 is:

> "...to administer a national network of lands and waters for the conservation, management, and where appropriate, restoration of the fish, wildlife and plant resources and their habitats within the United States for the benefit of present and future generations of Americans."

The National Wildlife Refuge System Improvement Act of 1997 (Improvement Act) established, for the first time, a clear legislative mission of wildlife conservation for the Refuge System. Actions were initiated in 1997 to comply with the direction of this new legislation, including an effort to complete comprehensive conservation plans for all refuges. These plans, which are completed with full public involvement, help guide the future management of refuges by establishing natural resources and recreation/education programs. Consistent with the Improvement Act, approved plans will serve as the guidelines for refuge management for the next 15 years. The Improvement Act states that each refuge shall be managed to:

- Fulfill the mission of the Refuge System;
- Fulfill the individual purposes of each refuge;
- Consider the needs of wildlife first;
- Fulfill requirements of comprehensive conservation plans that are prepared for each unit of the Refuge System;
- Maintain the biological integrity, diversity, and environmental health of the Refuge System; and
- Recognize that wildlife-dependent recreation activities, including hunting, fishing, wildlife observation, wildlife photography, and environmental education and interpretation, are legitimate and priority public uses; and allow refuge managers authority to determine compatible public uses.

The following are just a few examples of your national network of conservation lands. Pelican Island National Wildlife Refuge, the first refuge, was established in 1903 for the protection of colonial nesting birds in Florida, such as the snowy egret and the brown pelican. Western refuges were established for American bison (1906), elk (1912), prong-horned antelope (1931), and desert bighorn sheep (1936) after over-hunting, competition with cattle, and natural disasters decimated once-abundant herds. The drought conditions of the 1930s Dust Bowl severely depleted breeding populations of ducks and geese. Refuges established during the Great Depression focused on waterfowl production areas (i.e., protection of prairie wetlands in America's heartland). The emphasis on waterfowl continues today but also includes protection of wintering habitat in response to a dramatic loss of bottomland hardwoods. By 1973, the Service had begun to focus on establishing refuges for endangered species.

Recreational visits to national wildlife refuges generate substantial economic activity. In 2006, 34.8 million visited refuges in the lower 48 states for recreation. Their spending generated almost $1.7 billion of sales in regional economies. In a study completed in 2002 on 15 refuges, visitation had grown 36 percent in 7 years. At the same time, the number of jobs generated in surrounding communities grew to 120 per refuge, up from 87 jobs in 1995, pouring more than $2.2 million into local economies. The 15 refuges in the study were Chincoteague (Virginia); National Elk (Wyoming); Crab Orchard (Illinois); Eufaula (Alabama); Charles M. Russell (Montana); Umatilla (Oregon); Quivira (Kansas); Mattamuskeet (North Carolina); Upper Souris (North Dakota); San Francisco Bay (California); Laguna Atacosa (Texas); Horicon (Wisconsin); Las Vegas (Nevada); Tule Lake (California); and Tensas River (Louisiana). Other findings also validate the belief that communities near refuges benefit economically. Expenditures on food, lodging, and transportation grew to $6.8 million per refuge, up 31 percent from $5.2 million in 1995. For each federal dollar spent on the Refuge System, surrounding communities benefited with $4.43 in recreation expenditures and $1.42 in job-related income (Caudill and Laughland, unpubl. data).

Volunteers continue to be a major contributor to the success of the Refuge System. In 2005, 37,996 volunteers contributed more than 1.5 million hours on refuges nationwide, a service valued at more than $26 million.

The wildlife and habitat vision for national wildlife refuges stresses that wildlife comes first; that ecosystems, biodiversity, and wilderness are vital concepts in refuge management; that refuges must be healthy and growth must be strategic; and that the Refuge System serves as a model for habitat management with broad participation from others.

The Improvement Act stipulates that comprehensive conservation plans be prepared in consultation with adjoining federal, state, and private landowners and that the Service should develop and implement a process to ensure an opportunity for active public involvement in the preparation and revision (every 15 years) of the plans.

All lands of the Refuge System will be managed in accordance with an approved comprehensive conservation plan that will guide management decisions and set forth strategies for achieving refuge unit purposes. The plan will be consistent with sound resource management principles, practices, and legal mandates, including Service compatibility standards and other Service policies, guidelines, and planning documents (602 FW 1.1).

LEGAL AND POLICY CONTEXT

Legal Mandates, Administrative and Policy Guidelines, and Other Special Considerations

Administration of national wildlife refuges is guided by the mission and goals of the Refuge System, congressional legislation, presidential executive orders, and international treaties. Policies for management options of refuges are further refined by administrative guidelines established by the Secretary of the Interior and by policy guidelines established by the Director of the Fish and Wildlife Service. Select legal summaries of treaties and laws relevant to administration of the Refuge System and management of the Mandalay NWR are provided in Appendix C.

Treaties, laws, administrative guidelines, and policy guidelines assist the refuge manager in making decisions pertaining to soil, water, air, flora, fauna, and other natural resources; historical and cultural resources; research and recreation on refuge lands; and provide a framework for cooperation between Mandalay NWR and other partners, such as The Nature Conservancy, the Trust for Public Lands, U.S. Geological Survey, Louisiana State University, the Black Bear Conservation Committee, and private landowners, etc.

Lands within the Refuge System are closed to public use unless specifically and legally opened. No refuge use may be allowed unless it is determined to be appropriate and compatible. The refuge manager determines if a use is appropriate based on sound professional judgment; uses that are illegal, inconsistent with existing policy, or unsafe may not be found appropriate. When a use is found appropriate, it must then be determined to be compatible before it is allowed on a refuge. A compatible use is a use that, in the sound professional judgment of the refuge manager, will not materially interfere with or detract from the fulfillment of the mission of the Refuge System or the purposes of the refuge. All programs and uses must be evaluated based on mandates set forth in the Improvement Act. Those mandates are to:

- Contribute to ecosystem goals, as well as refuge purposes and goals;
- Conserve, manage, and restore fish, wildlife, and plant resources and their habitats;
- Monitor the trends of fish, wildlife, and plants;
- Manage and ensure appropriate visitor uses as those uses benefit the conservation of fish and wildlife resources and contribute to the enjoyment of the public; and
- Ensure that visitor activities are compatible with refuge purposes.

The Improvement Act further identifies six priority wildlife-dependent recreational uses. These uses are: hunting, fishing, wildlife observation, wildlife photography, and environmental education and interpretation. As priority public uses of the Refuge System, they receive priority consideration over other public uses in planning and management.

Biological Integrity, Diversity, and Environmental Health Policy

The Improvement Act directs the Service to ensure that the biological integrity, diversity, and environmental health of the Refuge System are maintained for the benefit of present and future generations of Americans. The policy is an additional directive for refuge managers to follow while achieving refuge purpose(s) and the Refuge System mission. It provides for the consideration and protection of the broad spectrum of fish, wildlife, and habitat resources found on refuges and associated ecosystems. When evaluating the appropriate management direction for refuges, refuge managers will use sound professional judgment to determine their refuges' contribution to biological integrity, diversity, and environmental health at multiple landscape scales. Sound professional judgment incorporates field experience, knowledge of refuge resources, refuge role within an ecosystem, applicable laws, and best available science, including consultation with others both inside and outside the Service.

The Energy Policy Act of 2005

The Energy Policy Act of 2005 (Public Law 109-58) was signed into law by President Bush on August 8, 2005. Section 384 of the Act establishes the Coastal Impact Assistance Program (CIAP), which authorizes funds to be distributed to Outer Continental Shelf oil and gas producing states to mitigate the impacts of Outer Continental Shelf oil and gas activities. States to share these funds are Alabama, Alaska, California, Louisiana, Mississippi, and Texas. (See further discussion below under conservation plans and initiatives.)

NATIONAL AND INTERNATIONAL CONSERVATION PLANS AND INITIATIVES

Multiple partnerships have been developed among government and private entities to address the environmental problems affecting regions. There is a large amount of conservation and protection information that defines the role of the refuge at the local, national, international, and ecosystem levels. Conservation initiatives include broad-scale planning and cooperation between affected parties to address declining trends of natural, physical, social, and economic environments. The conservation guidance described below, along with issues, problems, and trends, was reviewed and integrated where appropriate into this CCP.

This CCP supports, among others, the Partners-in-Flight Plan, the North American Waterfowl Management Plan, the Western Hemisphere Shorebird Reserve Network, and the National Wetlands Priority Conservation Plan.

North American Bird Conservation Initiative. Started in 1999, the North American Bird Conservation Initiative is a coalition of government agencies, private organizations, academic institutions, and private industry leaders in the United States, Canada, and Mexico, working to ensure the long-term health of North America's native bird populations by fostering an integrated approach to bird conservation to benefit all birds in all habitats. The four international and national bird initiatives include the North American Waterfowl Management Plan, Partners-in-Flight, Waterbird Conservation for the Americas, and the U.S. Shorebird Conservation Plan.

North American Waterfowl Management Plan. The North American Waterfowl Management Plan is an international action plan to conserve migratory birds throughout the continent. The plan's goal is to return waterfowl populations to their 1970s levels by conserving wetland and upland habitat. Canada and the United States signed the plan in 1986 in reaction to critically low numbers of waterfowl. Mexico joined in 1994, making it a truly continental effort. The plan is a partnership of federal, provincial/state and municipal governments, non-governmental organizations, private companies, and many individuals, all working towards achieving better wetland habitat for the benefit of migratory birds, other wetland-associated species and people. Plan projects are international in scope, but implemented at regional levels. These projects contribute to the protection of habitat and wildlife species across the North American landscape.

Partners-in-Flight Bird Conservation Plan. Managed as part of the Partners-in-Flight Plan, the Coastal Prairies physiographic area represents a scientifically based land bird conservation planning effort that ensures long-term maintenance of healthy populations of native land birds, primarily non-game land birds. Non-game land birds have been vastly under-represented in conservation efforts, and many are exhibiting significant declines. This plan is voluntary and non-regulatory, and focuses on relatively common species in areas where conservation actions can be most effective, rather than the frequent local emphasis on rare and peripheral populations.

U.S. Shorebird Conservation Plan. The U.S. Shorebird Conservation Plan is a partnership effort throughout the United States to ensure that stable and self-sustaining populations of shorebird species are restored and protected. The plan was developed by a wide range of agencies, organizations, and shorebird experts for separate regions of the country, and identifies conservation goals, critical habitat conservation needs, key research needs, and proposed education and outreach programs to increase awareness of shorebirds and the threats they face.

Northern American Waterbird Conservation Plan. This plan provides a framework for the conservation and management of 210 species of waterbirds in 29 nations. Threats to waterbird populations include destruction of inland and coastal wetlands, introduced predators and invasive species, pollutants, mortality from fisheries and industries, disturbance, and conflicts arising from abundant species. Particularly important habitats of the southeast region include pelagic areas, marshes, forested wetlands, and barrier and sea island complexes. Fifteen species of waterbirds are federally listed, including breeding populations of wood storks, Mississippi sandhill cranes, whooping cranes, interior least terns, and Gulf Coast populations of brown pelicans. A key objective of this plan is the standardization of data collection efforts to better recommend effective conservation measures.

Coastal Impact Assistance Program (CIAP). A Federal law, signed in 2005, authorizes the Secretary of the Interior to distribute $250 million for each of the fiscal years 2007 through 2010 to oil and gas producing States (Alabama, Alaska, California, Louisiana, Mississippi, and Texas) and coastal political subdivisions to be used for one or more of the following purposes:

- Projects and activities for the conservation, protection, or restoration of coastal areas, including wetlands.
- Mitigation of damage to fish, wildlife, or natural resources.
- Planning assistance and the administrative costs of complying with this section.
- Implementation of a federally approved marine, coastal or comprehensive conservation management plan.
- Mitigation of the impact of Outer Continental Shelf activities through funding or onshore infrastructure projects and public service needs.

In a Continuing Resolution dated February 16, 2007, Congress approved a 3 percent appropriation of the CIAP funds to be used by Minerals Management Service (MMS) to administer the CIAP program. MMS will lead the CIAP by establishing an environment that will enhance partner communications and an effective business relationship. Each eligible State will be allocated its share based on the State's Qualified Outer Continental Shelf Revenue generated off of its coast in proportion to total revenue generated off the coasts of all eligible states. MMS will respond to recipients needs and provide advice through guidance, direction, training, and by ensuring that monitoring and evaluation are incorporated into a system of accountability designed to accomplish the results intended by the Energy Policy Act of 2005.

REGIONAL CONSERVATION PLANS AND INITIATIVES

In the Louisiana Comprehensive Wildlife Conservation Strategy, developed in 2005 by the Louisiana Department of Wildlife and Fisheries (LDWF), Mandalay NWR is located in the Gulf Coast Prairies and Marshes ecoregion and the Terrebonne management basin. LDWF's strategy states that fresh marsh habitat, which occurs on Mandalay NWR, is the marsh type that has undergone the largest reduction in acreage of any of the marsh types over the past 20 years. LDWF lists 31 species as state species of conservation concern that depend on this habitat type. Cypress-tupelo swamp habitat, another predominant habitat on Mandalay NWR, is recognized as threatened by land loss caused by subsidence, altered hydrology, coastal erosion, and saltwater intrusion. Eighteen species are listed as state species of conservation concern in this habitat.

The Coastal Wetlands Planning, Protection and Restoration Act program (CWPPRA or "Breaux Act") provides for targeted funds to be used for planning and implementing projects that create, protect, restore and enhance wetlands in coastal Louisiana. Passed in 1990 and authorized until 2019, the federal funds created by this act are managed by the CWPPRA Task Force, a group composed of five Federal agencies, including the Service, and the State of Louisiana.

To address larger wetland restoration projects with more ecosystem-scale impacts than CWPPRA, the Louisiana Coastal Area Ecosystem Restoration Study (LCA) began in 2001. LCA seeks future Water Resources Development Act (WRDA) authorization and funding to identify critical human and natural ecological needs for coastal Louisiana, seeks alternatives to meet the needs including restoration priorities, and presents long-term large-scale strategies named the LCA Plan. Mandalay NWR are located in the Deltaic Plain area of LCA.

Coast 2050: Toward a Sustainable Coastal Louisiana was approved in 1998 by the State of Louisiana and its Federal partners. Coast 2050 is a joint planning initiative among the Louisiana Wetland Conservation and Restoration Authority, Louisiana Department of Natural Resources (DNR) Coastal Zone Management (CZM) Authority, and the CWPPRA Task Force for protecting and sustaining the state's coastal resources for future generations in a manner consistent with the welfare of the people. In this plan, Mandalay NWR are located in Region 3 (Terrebonne, Atchafalaya, Teche/Vermilion). The plan emphasizes that immediate attention should be placed in the Barataria Basin with ecosystem strategies to restore swamps, restore and sustain marshes, protect bay/lake shorelines, and restore barrier islands and Gulf shorelines.

In 1989, the Louisiana Legislature passed Act 6 (LA R.S. 49:213.1 et seq. of the Second Extraordinary Session of the Legislature), recognizing the catastrophic nature of Louisiana's coastal land loss and expanded the state's capacity to respond to the crisis by creating the Wetlands Conservation and Restoration Authority (State Wetlands Authority); the Wetlands Conservation and Restoration Fund (the Fund); the Governor's Office of Coastal Activities (GOCA); and the Office of Coastal Restoration and Management. The State Wetlands Authority is a policy level decision making group made up of the Governor's Executive Assistant for Coastal Activities, the Commissioner of the Division of Administration, and the secretaries of five state agencies - the Department of Wildlife and Fisheries, Environmental Quality, Natural Resources, Transportation and Development, and Agriculture and Forestry. The State Wetlands Authority is the sponsor and official author of the State Plan, an annual summary of coastal restoration projects and recommendations for funding from the Fund. The Fund's income is from a portion of the state's mineral income and severance taxes from oil and gas production on state lands and is dedicated to state sponsored coastal restoration projects. The GOCA coordinates policy among the many agencies involved in Louisiana's coastal restoration effort, while the Office of Coastal Restoration and Management within DNR handles day-to-day implementation of coastal restoration in coordination with the Coastal Zone Management Office.

LOWER MISSISSIPPI RIVER VALLEY ECOSYSTEM

Mandalay NWR lies within a physiographic region designated by the Service as the Lower Mississippi River Ecosystem (LMRE). The LMRE serves as the primary wintering habitat for mid-continent waterfowl populations, as well as breeding and migration habitat for migratory songbirds returning from Central and South America. Geographically, the refuge lies in the southern part of the LMRE. Mandalay NWR has opportunities to contribute to many of the goals and objectives of the LMRE. The following goals of the LMRE are applicable to the refuge:

- Conserve, enhance, protect, and monitor migratory bird populations and their habitats in the LMRE;
- Protect, restore, and manage the wetlands of the LMRE;
- Protect and/or restore imperiled habitats and viable populations of all threatened, endangered, and candidate species and species of concern in the LMRE;
- Protect, restore, and manage the fisheries and other aquatic resources historically associated with the wetlands and waters of the LMRE;
- Restore, manage, and protect national wildlife refuges and national fish hatcheries;
- Increase public awareness and support for LMRE resources and their management;
- Enforce natural resource laws; and
- Protect, restore, and enhance water and air quality throughout the LMRE.

National wildlife refuges in the Lower Mississippi Valley (LMV) serve as part of the last safety net to support biological diversity – the greatest challenge facing the Service. According to the LMRE Team, the greatest threats to biological diversity within the LMV include:

- The loss of sustainable communities, including the loss of 20 million acres of bottomland hardwood forests;
- The loss of connectivity between bottomland hardwood forest sites (e.g., forest fragmentation);
- The effects of agricultural and timber harvesting practices;
- The simplification of the remaining wildlife habitats within the ecosystem and gene pools;
- The effects of constructing navigation and water diversion projects; and
- The cumulative habitat effects of land and water resource development activities.

Priorities identified by the LMRE to which the refuge can contribute include:

- Continue to work with the Louisiana Coastal Wetlands Task Force, private landowners, and other entities to protect and restore coastal wetlands, consistent with the Coast 2050 Plan and associated project planning, evaluation, and implementation activities;
- Consider all grant opportunities available to the LMRE Team and partners and work to improve internal coordination of these programs to assure that the contributions to these programs are of maximum benefit to the resource;
- Support environmental education efforts underway by Service offices to enhance and expand knowledge, awareness, and appreciation of trust resources; and
- Control invasive/exotic species.

RELATIONSHIP TO STATE WILDLIFE AGENCY

A provision of the Improvement Act, and subsequent agency policy, is that the Service shall ensure timely and effective cooperation and collaboration with other state fish and game agencies and tribal governments during the course of acquiring and managing refuges. State wildlife management areas and national wildlife refuges provide the foundation for the protection of species, and contribute to the overall health and sustainability of fish and wildlife species in the State of Louisiana.

In Louisiana, the Louisiana Department of Wildlife and Fisheries (LDWF) is vested with responsibility for conservation and management of wildlife in the state, including aquatic life, and is authorized to execute the laws enacted for the control and supervision of programs relating to the management, protection, conservation, and replenishment of wildlife, fish, and aquatic life, and the regulation of the shipping of wildlife fish, furs, and skins. LDWF's mission is to manage, conserve, and promote wise utilization of Louisiana's renewable fish and wildlife resources and their supporting habitats through replenishment, protection, enhancement, research, development, and education for the social and economic benefit of current and future generations; to provide opportunities for knowledge of and use and enjoyment of these resources; and to promote a safe and healthy environment for the users of the resources. LDWF is divided into seven divisions for management of the state's resources: Enforcement, Coastal and Nongame Resources, Public Information, Inland Fisheries, Marine Fisheries, Management and Finance, and Wildlife.

The participation of LDWF throughout this comprehensive conservation planning process has been valuable. Not only have LDWF personnel participated in the biological reviews, they are also active partners in annual hunt coordination, planning, and various wildlife and habitat surveys. A key part of the planning process is the integration of common objectives between the Service and LDWF. Several LDWF wildlife management areas are located near Mandalay NWR (Figure 2).

The state's participation and contribution throughout this planning process will provide for ongoing opportunities and open dialogue to improve the ecological sustainability of fish and wildlife in the State of Louisiana. An essential part of comprehensive conservation planning is integrating common mission objectives where appropriate.

Figure 2. Location of Mandalay National Wildlife Refuge in relation to regional conservation areas

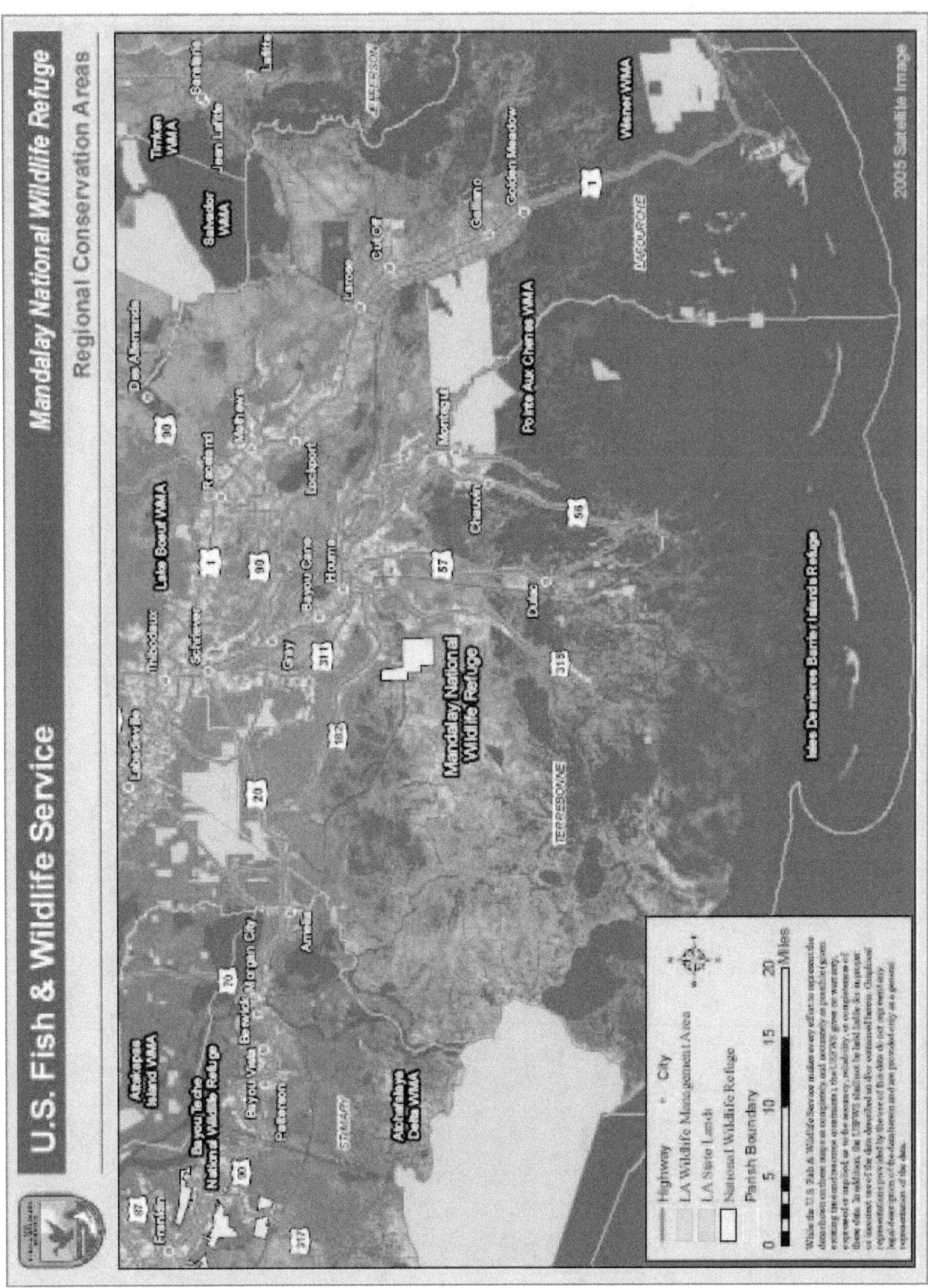

II. Refuge Overview

INTRODUCTION

Mandalay NWR is approximately 5 miles west of Houma, Louisiana, in Terrebonne Parish (Figures 3, 4, and 5). The refuge consists predominantly of freshwater marshes and cypress-tupelo swamps, which provide excellent habitat for waterfowl, wading birds, and neotropical songbirds. Access is by boat, except for the headquarters building on Highway 182 (Bayou Black Drive) and a nearby nature trail. Mandalay NWR is administered as one of eight refuges of the Southeast Louisiana National Wildlife Refuge Complex, Lacombe, Louisiana.

MANDALAY REFUGE HISTORY AND PURPOSE

Mandalay NWR was established on May 2, 1996, with the purchase of 4,416 acres under the authority of the Migratory Bird Conservation Act of 1929 and the Endangered Species Act of 1973. The refuge's establishment was the culmination of supportive efforts from many conservation organizations, including the Louisiana Nature Conservancy (LNC), the National Fish and Wildlife Foundation, and the North American Wetlands Council; and private companies and individuals, including Dow Chemical Company and Mr. Michael St. Martin.

In the beginning, the public was divisive in its support of the refuge's establishment. When the first notices, draft documents, and news releases announcing the proposed Mandalay NWR were made public in 1992, many negative public comments were received. Pre-written postcards by an individual opposing the project were circulated. Of the 468 pre-written postcards received, 64 percent (296) were opposed, 1 percent (6) was in support, and 35 percent (163) requested a hearing on the project.

The Service held a public hearing in December 1992 in Houma, Louisiana; more than 500 people attended. Issues of concern included: (1) Confusion between the proposed 15,000-acre Mandalay NWR and a 500,000-acre Bayou Penchant Basin Plan, a non-acquisition basin-wide management project which had no direct ties to the refuge; (2) that refuge establishment would result in a loss of revenue from the local real estate tax base; (3) that the Service would initiate a basin-wide "land grab" through condemnation or eminent domain; (4) that the Service would exclude oil and gas operations or impose more restrictions on oil and gas production with the refuge; (5) that access for hunting and fishing in the area would be lost; and, (6) there was local confidence that the current landowners were doing a good job in managing and protecting the wetlands and wildlife resources in the area.

At the close of the extended public comment period after the hearing, 1,014 responses were received. Of this total, 22 percent (227) supported the proposed refuge establishment; 53 percent (533) opposed it; 22 percent (227) requested that the Service "shelve" the project pending changes in local public opinion; and 3 percent (27) commented without indicating support or opposition. Again, most of the responses opposing the project were from pre-typed letter and postcard campaigns. In a number of cases, some individuals signed and sent multiple copies of the Xeroxed form letter; in other cases, a few individuals signed the names and addresses of other people. Only 46 letters were personally written by individuals opposing the project. The Service received a total of 202 written letters supporting the project.

Figure 3. Status and acquisition boundary of Mandalay National Wildlife Refuge, Terrebonne Parish, LA and vicinity (topo)

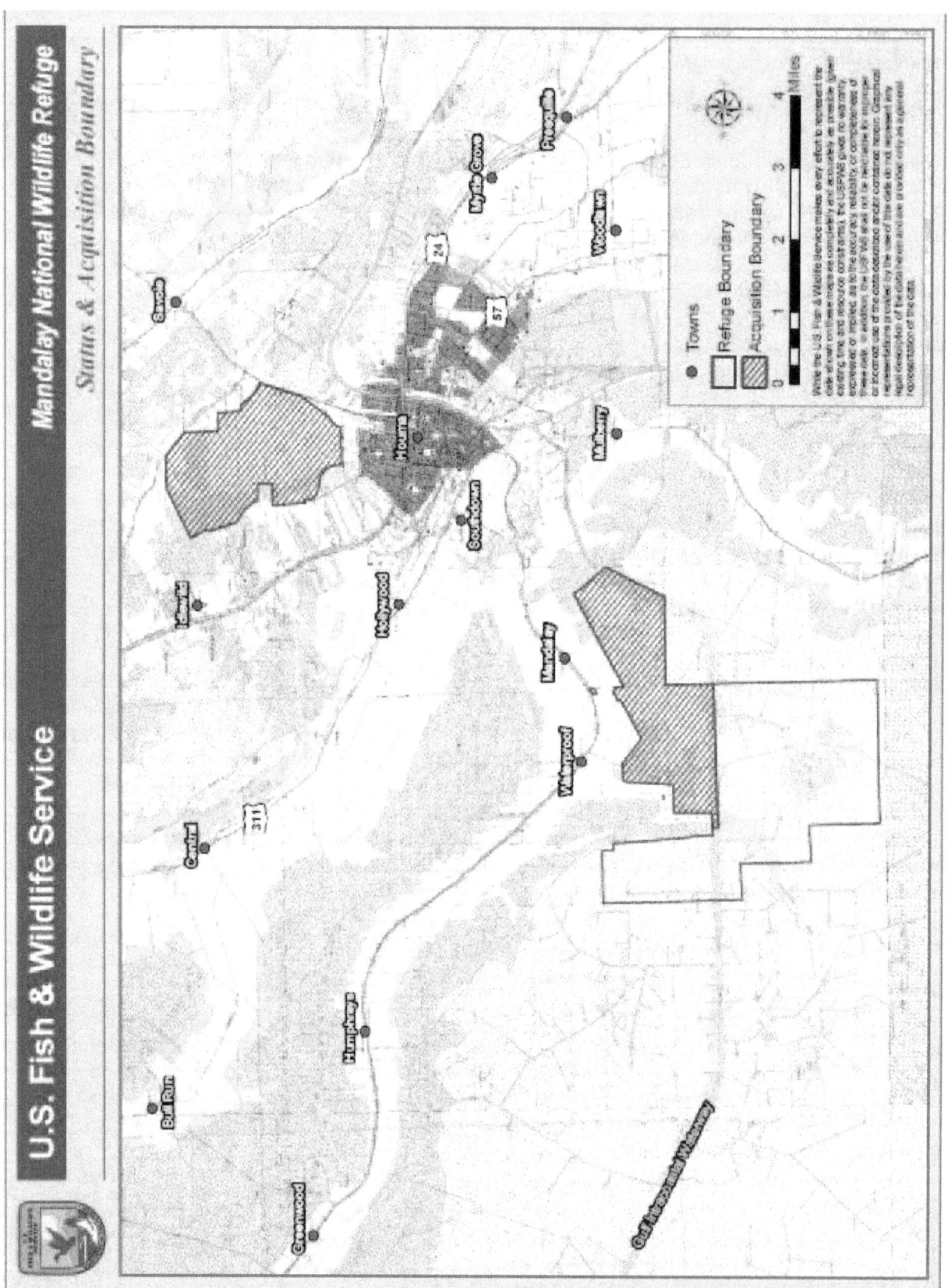

Figure 4. Status and acquisition boundary of Mandalay National Wildlife Refuge, Terrebonne Parish, LA, and vicinity

Figure 5. Boundary of Mandalay National Wildlife Refuge, Terrebonne Parish, LA

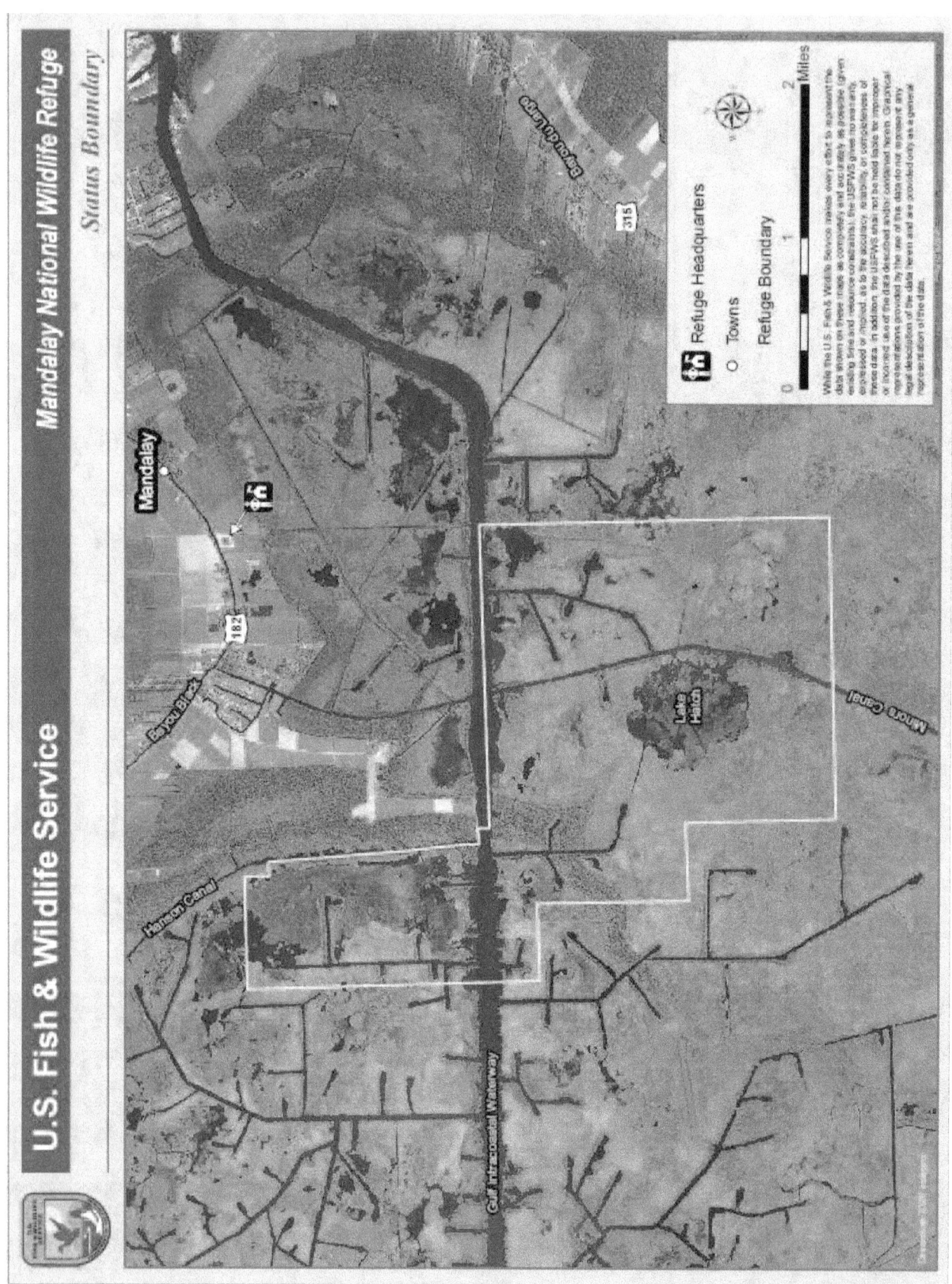

The concerns and issues of the community were numerous and complex. The Final Environmental Assessment for the Proposed Establishment of Mandalay National Wildlife Refuge provides additional details on the issues and concerns regarding the proposed refuge and how they were addressed. In brief, the Final Environmental Assessment completed in 1995, recognized and took the concerns into consideration.

In 1994, the Terrebonne Parish Council (Council) formed the Lake Houma Advisory Committee to study the feasibility of federal acquisition and public recreation at Lake Houma. A preliminary study indicated that Lake Houma could possibly be acquired and managed in connection with the proposed Mandalay NWR, once the refuge was established. At a February 1995 meeting attended by the Service, the Lake Houma Advisory Committee, adjacent landowners, representatives of elected officials, and concerned citizens, there was general support for the establishment of the refuge, with the possible addition of Lake Houma in the future. Two public meetings were held by the Council in July and August 1995. During the public comment period, only one negative comment was received. In August 1995, the Council unanimously passed a resolution in full support of Mandalay NWR and the future Lake Houma proposal, and signed an agreement with the Service stating this support.

The purposes of Mandalay NWR, based upon land acquisition documents and its establishing authority, are as follows:

"... for use as an inviolate sanctuary, or for any other management purpose, for migratory birds. 16 U.S.C. 715d (Migratory Bird Conservation Act).

"... to conserve (A) fish or wildlife which are listed as endangered species or threatened species... or (B) plants..." 16 U.S.C. 1534 (Endangered Species Act of 1973).

SPECIAL DESIGNATIONS

Prior to Mandalay NWR's designation as a national wildlife refuge, this acreage was intensively developed by oil and gas companies. Currently, there is only one active gas well on the refuge. However, there is a gathering facility (Sunrise Canal), which has and will be used in the future to process and transport by pipeline and barge petroleum products from the refuge and surrounding areas. Current mineral owners are actively planning for additional exploration on and near the refuge. The refuge was previously owned by the Southdown Sugar Plantation, and was used for oil field operations and cattle grazing.

ECOLOGICAL THREATS AND PROBLEMS

The primary ecological threats to Mandalay NWR are land loss, invasive species, and the potential of contaminants from oil and gas operations. The refuge is in the Terrebonne Basin, which experienced land loss rates of 10.2 sq mi/yr (16.4 sq km/year) from 1978-1990. During this time, 61 percent of all Louisiana coastal land loss occurred within the Terrebonne and Barataria basins compared to the seven remaining Louisiana coastal hydrologic basins defined by the CWPPRA Task Force. Most of these losses were interior marshes with some non-fresh land losses skirting the bays. The refuge has experienced land losses from both internal marsh break-up and considerable shoreline erosion along the Gulf Intracoastal Waterway (GIWW). Additionally, the USGS has documented approximately 19 sq mi (49 sq km) of land lost from October 2004 to October 2005 in the Terrebonne Basin as measured following Hurricanes Katrina and Rita.

Mandalay NWR has several invasive plant and animal species which occur on the refuge that include but are not limited to hydrilla, common and giant salvinia, Eurasian watermilfoil, water hyacinth, Chinese tallow, nutria, and feral swine. These non-native species out-compete native species, are difficult to control, degrade water quality and cause access problems in the waterways.

The Sunrise Oil and Gas Field contains a gathering station headquartered on the refuge with flowlines to it from several wells off the refuge that supply raw petroleum to the station. The potential for spills, leaks, and contaminants exist. Maintenance of existing facilities, developing new structures for mineral extraction, and spills including clean up operations have the potential to adversely affect wetlands. There are numerous oil and gas pipelines that traverse the refuge. The Southeast Louisiana National Wildlife Refuge Complex Contingency Plan will be utilized to address any such spill occurrences.

PHYSICAL RESOURCES

CLIMATE

The climate in southern Louisiana is humid and subtropical with long, hot summers. The fall and spring are warm and often free of killing frost. Winters are usually mild and cool, but temperatures occasionally drop to the lower teens. The lowest recorded in recent history was 10° F.; the average frost-free period is 264 days and extends from February 27 to November 18. The average annual rainfall is 65 inches, but amounts exceeding 87 inches have been recorded. Tropical disturbances and hurricanes occur often and can cause changes in salinity and storm related flooding.

The Intergovernmental Panel on Climate Change (IPCC) recently concluded that warming of the climate is undeniable. Coasts are projected to be exposed to increasing risks, including coastal erosion, due to climate change and sea-level rise and the effect will be exacerbated by increasing human-induced pressures on coastal areas. Coastal wetlands are projected to be negatively affected by sea-level rise.

In an effort to address the potential effects of sea level rise on national wildlife refuges, the Service contracted the application of the Sea Level Affecting Marshes Model (SLAMM) for most Region 4 refuges (SLAMM Report for Mandalay NWR 2008).

Simulation results suggest that tidal freshwater marsh will be at least 95 percent lost under all scenarios; it is predominantly a question of when. The loss is gradual with 95 percent of tidal freshwater marsh being lost by 2100. Although under the 1 and 1.5 meter scenarios, 90 percent and nearly 100 percent is lost by 2050 respectively. Inland freshwater marsh follows much the same pattern but the loss rate is greater in most cases. Swamps are actually predicted to fare worse than freshwater marshes in these simulations, being 99 to 100 percent lost by the year 2100 under even the most moderate scenario run. Within the SLAMM model, swamps are not predicted to vertically accrete as quickly as marshes do. Under all but the most extreme scenarios, migration of saltwater marsh into Mandalay NWR is predicted.

GEOLOGY, HYDROLOGY, AND TOPOGRAPHY

Mandalay NWR is located within the Terrebonne Basin, an abandoned delta complex, characterized by a thick section of unconsolidated sediments and a network of old distributary ridges extending southward from Houma. The refuge lies within the Penchant Sub-basin and receives freshwater from the hydrologic influences of the Atchafalaya River. The northern Penchant Sub-basin supports extensive freshwater marsh and includes a predominance of flotant marsh. In recent years, the Penchant Sub-basin has experienced significant freshwater impacts from the Atchafalaya River. Historic wetlands loss resulting from subsidence, saltwater intrusion, and oil and gas activity appears to have moderated, but areas of cypress swamp and flotant marsh are experiencing stress from high water levels. The lands of the refuge consist of freshwater marshes, swamps, upland ridges, bayous, and other bodies of water.

SOILS

The ridge soils of Mandalay NWR are predominantly Fausse clay and Cancienne silty clay loam. The marsh soils are organic and mucky, and are affected by some sediment recharge from the Atchafalaya River. Soil types are predominantly Kenner muck (very frequently flooded) and Allemands muck (very frequently flooded).

BIOLOGICAL RESOURCES

HABITAT

The main habitats of Mandalay NWR include freshwater marshes intersected by a major ridge with associated swamp borders. The refuge contains 3,700 acres of freshwater marshes, 75 acres of bordering swamps, 175 acres of upland ridges, and various oil-field canals and other water bodies. Lake Hatch, approximately 200 acres, is the single largest water body on the refuge.

The marsh habitat north of the GIWW consists predominantly of bull-tongue. Other freshwater plants include pickerel weed, maidencane, alligatorweed, pennywort, lotus, white waterlily, primrose, water hyacinth, cattail, bulrush, beggartick, cut-grass, spikerush, and several species of sedges. The marsh vegetation south of the GIWW is much the same, but maidencane is dominant. Submerged plants, such as cabomba, coontail, hydrilla, and pondweed, are common.

The small acreage of higher ground supports a hardwood forest that is an extremely important component of the refuge. The natural levee and spoil banks of the man-made canals are vegetated by black willow, hackberry, Nuttall oak, water oak, green ash, and swamp red maple. Low swamp areas are dominated by cypress and tupelo gum. The canals are lined by willow and cypress. Buttonbush is common in the intergradational areas between swamp and marsh.

Mandalay NWR provides productive freshwater fish habitat as well as nursery grounds for commercial fish and shellfish found in the Gulf of Mexico.

WILDLIFE

The refuge provides excellent habitat for wintering waterfowl of the Mississippi Flyway. The most common wintering waterfowl species include blue-winged teal, green-winged teal, American widgeon, ring-necked duck, lesser scaup, mallard, gadwall, and northern pintail. Resident waterfowl species include wood ducks, mottled ducks, and black-bellied whistling ducks.

Mandalay NWR and surrounding areas provide important shallow water and mudflat habitat for shorebirds, particularly during the critical fall migration periods. The variety of emergent marsh habitats are thought to support a significant number of waterbirds. The highest priority species are king rail, clapper rail, pied-billed grebe, least bittern, American bittern, and purple gallinule. Marsh birds depend on the erect emergent, herbaceous vegetation and intermingled mud flats for cover, foraging, and nesting.

While several species of wading birds are commonly observed foraging in the shallow water habitats on the refuge, priority species occurring include little blue heron, tricolored heron, yellow-crowned night heron, wood stork, and white ibis. Usage of the refuge by gulls and terns is minimal.

The areas of forestland protruding into the marshes are important for trans-Gulf migrating songbirds and are important nesting sites for prothonotary warblers.

Although Mandalay NWR is primarily a refuge dedicated to the management and protection of migratory birds, it currently supports a population of white-tailed deer that appears to be of relatively low density. Squirrels and rabbits are the two primary small game animals on the refuge. The refuge supports a significant population of furbearers including raccoon, otter, muskrat, mink and bobcat. Native furbearers have declined as the nutria has become established in the region. Feral hogs are also prolific.

Although no herpetological surveys have been conducted to date on refuge lands, commonly seen species of reptiles and amphibians include alligators, alligator snapping turtles, eastern box turtles, water moccasins, eastern mud snakes, bullfrogs, pig frogs, Southern leopard frogs, and Gulf Coast toads. The marshes of the refuge provide nursery grounds for many fish and shellfish. Freshwater fish such as largemouth bass, crappie, sunfish, and catfish provide sport fishing opportunities.

CULTURAL RESOURCES

The first inhabitants of Terrebonne Parish were unknown Native Americans dating back hundreds of years ago. Some people claim the Houmas Indians were the original inhabitants of Terrebonne Parish, but they actually arrived in the mid- to late-18th century from Mississippi and Alabama. The native word "houma" means red, and the tribe's war emblem was the crawfish. The tribe was pushed from the higher ground to the coastal regions by European settlements in the late 1700s and 1800s. The explorer LaSalle claimed Louisiana for France in 1682, but it was Iberville that actually brought settlers in 1699. The first settlers were mostly of French ancestry, either from France or the Acadians from Nova Scotia. The early French settlers called this area "terre bonne," which means good earth, because of the fertility of the soil and abundance of fish and wildlife. Most of the pioneers who came to Terrebonne migrated from the Mississippi River, down Bayou Lafourche to Bayou Terrebonne. They chose the area because of its isolated geographic location, minimum government controls, and the abundant resources that made it easy to live off the land. During Spain's domination in the mid - 1700s, both Spanish and Anglo-Saxons recorded land claims in the area. The Louisiana territory was purchased by the United States in 1803, causing another large influx of colonists.

The Final Environmental Assessment for the proposed establishment of Mandalay NWR identified 10 known prehistoric sites within the boundaries of the proposed refuge, and states that other sites may exist. Any future plans or actions that might affect eligible cultural resources will be carried out according to the National Historic Preservation Act of 1966, as amended.

SOCIOECONOMIC ENVIRONMENT

In the mid-1800s, industry consisted largely of farming plantations, seafood, fur trading, and logging, with sugar cane being the principal agricultural industry. Canals were dug to decrease travel time and to make trade more efficient. These canals were later abandoned with the construction of the Intracoastal Waterway in 1923. The oil and gas industry began in the 1920s and brought a period of economic development and prosperity that became the main economic focus of the area until the bottom fell out of the oil industry in the early 1980s. Since that time the Houma community has begun to diversify. While the oil industry is still the primary source of revenue, alternative industries are emerging, such as seafood production, medical businesses, and tourism, which have become popular sources of commerce.

REFUGE ADMINISTRATION AND MANAGEMENT

LAND PROTECTION AND CONSERVATION

The major management activities on Mandalay NWR include wetland restoration projects, control of invasive species, law enforcement, wood duck nest box program, wildlife monitoring, and oil and gas operation monitoring. Marsh restoration projects on the refuge include the Mandalay Bank Protection Demonstration CWPPRA project along the southern shoreline of the GIWW, and the Hanson Marsh Hydrologic Restoration NAWCA project. Exotic and invasive species have been recognized as a habitat management challenge on the refuge since its establishment.

Law enforcement issues involve patrolling the refuge for unauthorized activities such illegal hunting, commercial fishing, and littering, as well as activities occurring when the refuge is closed at night. Monitoring of wildlife is limited to monthly winter waterfowl surveys, and an annual alligator night count. Approximately 20 wood duck boxes are maintained. Monitoring oil and gas activities requires planning and coordination with the oil and gas operators on the refuge. Duties involve not only emergency procedures and supervision during spills, but dealing with legal matters after spill events, and permitting and mitigating actions for ongoing activities such as pipeline routes (installation and removal), night activities, equipment use, drilling, seismic exploration, and plugging and abandoning structures.

VISITOR SERVICES

Visitor services consist of hunting and fishing opportunities, wildlife observation, and a nature trail; refuge information is available at refuge headquarters and online (Figure 6). All access to refuge land other than the refuge headquarters and the nature trail is by boat. Hunting opportunities at Mandalay NWR include an open archery deer and feral hog season and a lottery waterfowl hunt for youth and adults. The archery deer and feral hog hunts are held concurrently with the State of Louisiana deer season. Waterfowl hunts are held on Wednesdays and Saturdays during the Louisiana waterfowl hunting season, as well as two additional state youth waterfowl hunt days. The refuge has five waterfowl blinds in the Hanson Unit. Each blind has a maximum capacity of 3 hunters for a total of 15 hunters each day. Five groups are chosen for each hunt date by lottery drawing from applications received at the refuge office. Youths between the ages of 8 and 17 receive preference in the drawing. Currently, the refuge staff estimates that about 50 percent of the hunt day opportunities are used each year. Fishing is offered on the refuge year-round from sunrise to sunset. Most of the fishing occurs in Lake Hatch and in the numerous old oilfield access canals found on the refuge. The refuge has worked with a local landowner to establish a vehicle accessible nature trail near the refuge office that gives visitors a chance to see areas similar to some of the habitat found on the refuge.

PERSONNEL, OPERATIONS, AND MAINTENANCE

Presently, Mandalay NWR has a 2-person staff consisting of a refuge manager and a wildlife biologist, working out of the headquarters near Houma. They receive minimal assistance in areas such as law enforcement, maintenance, and visitor services, when needed, from other staff of the Southeast Louisiana NWR Complex. Mandalay NWR does have a separate refuge budget; funds and projects are supplemented by the Southeast Louisiana NWR Complex administration.

Figure 6. Public use areas and facilities on Mandalay National Wildlife Refuge

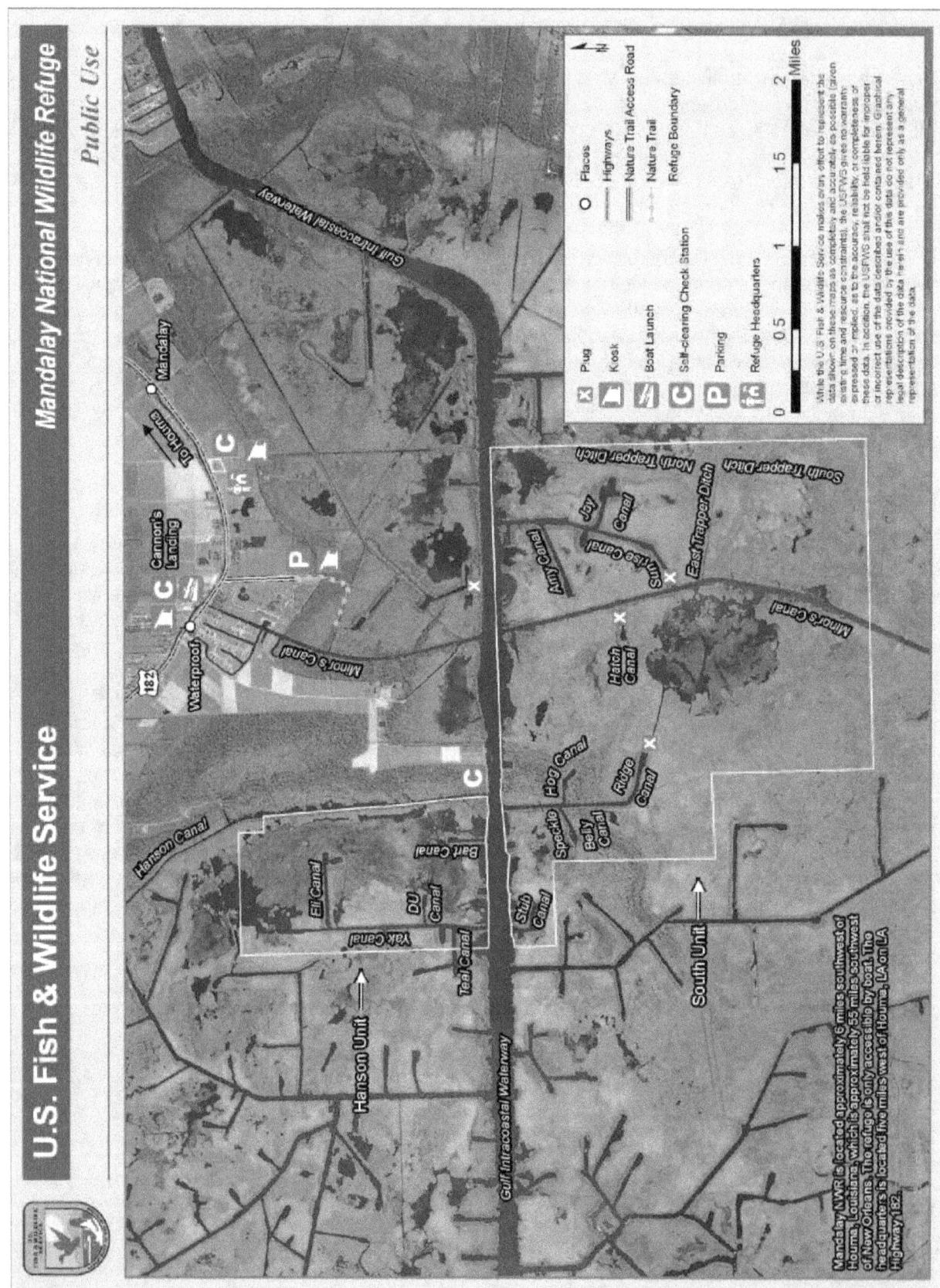

III. Plan Development

PLANNING PROCESS AND PUBLIC INVOLVEMENT

In October 2006, the planning process began with a biological review for Mandalay NWR to assess the status of current biological information and programs on the refuge, identify information gaps and needs, and gather input on potential management goals and objectives. Diverse teams consisting of Service, university, state, and non-governmental personnel were invited to attend and provide input. Issues discussed were marsh and forest management, aquatic systems, migratory birds, threatened and endangered species, non-game birds, mammals, reptiles and amphibians, insects, water quality, contaminants, urbanization, and land acquisition.

A visitor services review was conducted in November 2006 to provide guidance for managing the education and visitor services program and resulted in the development of short- to long-term recommendations to improve the quality of visitor experiences and understanding of the refuge. The review team was composed of staff and other professionals from the Service's Regional Office. General recommendations were to develop a visitor services plan, strengthen the volunteer program, and provide sufficient law enforcement.

Formal public involvement began with an open house held in April 2007 for the general public to give suggestions and comments regarding the future of the refuge. Announcements giving the location, date, and time for the scoping meeting appeared in local newspapers and were furnished to local residents. The public meeting for Mandalay NWR was held in Houma. Approximately 7 people attended the open discussion of the CCP process to learn about future management plans for Mandalay NWR. After orienting attendees to the CCP process, they could move freely among the following discussion areas: public programs and visitor facilities, wildlife and habitat management, and refuge administration. Each area offered information and a chance to make written and oral statements (Appendix D). Also, comment cards were available, which could be mailed to the refuge. Approximately 11 comments and questions were recorded for the Mandalay NWR meeting. Input obtained from the scoping meetings was used to develop the draft CCP. No major conflicts were declared in the comments received from the public.

Initial planning began in May 2007, with a meeting of planning team members. Early in the process of developing this CCP, the planning team identified a list of issues and concerns that were likely to be associated with the conservation and management of Mandalay NWR based on the reviews and public scoping. A mailing list of members of the public, landowners, state and tribal agencies, non-profit organizations, local governments, and other interested stakeholders was initiated.

WILDERNESS REVIEW

Refuge planning policy requires a wilderness review as part of the comprehensive conservation planning process. The lands within the boundary of Mandalay NWR were reviewed for their suitability in meeting the criteria for wilderness, as defined by the Wilderness Act of 1964. The refuge does not contain the required 5,000 contiguous road-less acres. Mandalay NWR comprises only 4,416 acres. Further, the proximity of the city of Houma, urban sprawl, and Louisiana Highway 182 detract from any semblance of a wilderness setting. Therefore, the suitability of refuge lands on Mandalay NWR for wilderness designation is not further analyzed in this CCP.

SUMMARY OF ISSUES, CONCERNS, AND OPPORTUNITIES

The planning team identified a number of issues, concerns, and opportunities related to fish and wildlife protection, habitat restoration, recreation and management of threatened and endangered species. Additionally, the planning team considered federal and state mandates, as well as applicable local ordinances, regulations, and plans. The team also directed the process of obtaining public input through public scoping meetings, written comments, and personal contacts. All public and advisory team comments were considered. The team considered all issues that were raised throughout the planning process, and this CCP attempts to balance the competing opinions regarding important issues. The team identified those issues that, in the team's best professional judgment, are most significant to the refuge. A summary of the significant issues follows.

FISH AND WILDLIFE POPULATION MANAGEMENT

The majority of issues pertaining to fish and wildlife populations on Mandalay NWR is discussed in the habitat management section, since managing habitat is the key to providing for the needs of fish and fauna. Because managing for migratory birds is one of the primary purposes of the refuge, maintaining migratory bird habitat is central to management actions. While limited waterfowl hunting is offered in some areas of the refuge, providing sanctuary for waterfowl during the hunting season is an important function of the refuge. Mandalay NWR is a relatively new refuge; continued monitoring of waterfowl populations during the winter and documenting usage of the refuge by other bird groups such as shorebirds, wading birds, raptors, and forest-dependent songbirds is needed.

Continued control of invasive and exotic species, such as nutria and feral hogs, is a significant management concern. Monitoring game species is a key component of population management and can be addressed by surveying and collecting harvest information on white-tailed deer and small game.

HABITAT MANAGEMENT

The land loss problem is one of the most important management issues, and predictions of continued erosion indicate that restoration efforts must be considered in the refuge's overall efforts to sustain the current ecological conditions. Overall productivity of the refuge seems high and maintaining existing habitats should be a higher priority than restoration, although restoring certain components, such as bank lines, marshes, and hydrologic conditions, may be required for protection of existing habitats. Efforts toward restoring refuge habitats should focus on the priorities of maintaining existing marshes and ridge habitats; restoring bank lines and marshes along waterways to protect existing wetlands; and maintaining habitat diversity through vegetation plantings in appropriate areas. Important issues to address are erosion along the Gulf Intracoastal Waterway, and floating, invasive species such as water hyacinth, common salvinia, and giant salvinia. Areas to consider for maintaining good waterfowl, shorebird, and marshbird habitat are the intact marshes on the south side of the Gulf Intracoastal Waterway, the open water in the Hanson Unit, and possibly creating islands in Lake Hatch, if material is available from dredging projects. Existing forests can be managed to provide resting and feeding habitat for songbirds, and can possibly be enhanced or expanded. Planting soft woods and/or fruit bearing trees, such as willow and sugarberry, will provide perching and foraging resources.

RESOURCE PROTECTION

The oil and gas operations on the refuge require monitoring by staff. Releases or spill events have the potential to impact waterfowl and other water birds and large expanses of habitat if not controlled immediately. Working with other agencies, staff must determine the best approaches to clean up spills.

VISITOR SERVICES

Hunting and fishing are traditional recreational uses in Louisiana and are the primary reasons the public visits the refuge. Archery deer and hog hunts are offered, as well as youth and adult lottery waterfowl hunts on specifically designated days, times, and areas. Fishing and recreational boating are permitted year-round from legal sunrise to legal sunset. Recreational crabbing is allowed. All access to the refuge is by boat except the refuge headquarters and a nearby nature trail, both located on Bayou Black Drive in Houma and accessible by vehicle. No public boat launches are located on the refuge. Under current funding and staffing, visitor services opportunities are limited.

REFUGE ADMINISTRATION

Presently, two positions cover the administration of both Mandalay and Bayou Teche NWR's from the headquarters in Houma. Limited support is available from the staff of Southeast Louisiana NWR Complex in Lacombe, a drive of several hours from Mandalay NWR. Funding is administered through the Southeast Louisiana NWR Complex.

IV. Management Direction

INTRODUCTION

The Service manages fish and wildlife habitats by considering the needs of all resources. First and foremost, fish and wildlife conservation assumes priority in refuge management. A requirement of the Improvement Act is for the Service to maintain the ecological health, diversity, and integrity of refuges. Public uses are allowed if they are appropriate and compatible with wildlife and habitat conservation, as well as the purposes for which the refuge was established. The Service has identified six priority wildlife-dependent public uses. These uses are: hunting, fishing, wildlife observation, wildlife photography, and environmental education and interpretation.

Described below is the CCP for managing the refuge over the next 15 years. This management direction contains the goals, objectives, and strategies that will be used to achieve the refuge vision.

Three alternatives for managing the refuge were considered:

A – No Action (Current Management)

B – Resource-Focused Management

C – User-Focused Management

Each of the alternatives is described in the Alternatives section of the Environmental Assessment, which was Section B of the draft CCP for Mandalay NWR. Based on the mission of the Refuge System, the purposes for which Mandalay NWR was established, and the focus of the LMRE priorities, the Service selected Alternative B as the preferred management direction.

Implementing the preferred alternative will result in a diversity of habitats for a variety of fish and wildlife species, enhance resident wildlife populations, restore wetlands, and provide opportunities for a variety of compatible wildlife-dependent recreation, education, and interpretive activities.

VISION

Mandalay National Wildlife Refuge will be managed as a productive freshwater marsh that provides essential wintering habitat for migratory birds along the Louisiana coast. The highest priority for the refuge will be to maintain prime waterfowl, shorebird, and wading bird habitat. The refuge will play a critical role in coastal restoration and erosion control efforts. This will be accomplished through agency coordination, to ensure quality coastal wetland habitat over the next 15 years. Mandalay NWR will provide the best possible habitat for mammalian, fish, amphibian, reptilian, and other avian species. Visitors to the refuge will enjoy a quality outdoor experience centered on the traditional uses of hunting and fishing, while cultivating a conservation ethic that promotes stewardship of important wildlife habitat.

GOALS, OBJECTIVES, AND STRATEGIES

The goals, objectives, and strategies presented are the Service's response to the issues, concerns and needs expressed by the planning team, the refuge staff, partners, and the public. Chapter VII, Plan Implementation, identifies the projects associated with the various strategies.

These goals, objectives, and strategies reflect the Service's commitment to achieve the mandates of the Improvement Act, the mission of the Refuge System, and the purposes and vision of Mandalay NWR. With resources as outlined in Chapter VII, we intend to accomplish these goals, objectives, and strategies within the next 15 years.

GOAL 1. Identify, conserve, manage, and restore populations of native fish and wildlife species representative of the Barataria-Terrebonne Basin, with emphasis on migratory birds and threatened and endangered species.

Background: The diversity and quality of habitats in Mandalay NWR provide areas for feeding, roosting, nesting, and staging for numerous bird species. The refuge attracts upwards of 20 species of migratory waterfowl (including 3 species of resident waterfowl), shorebirds, wading birds, neo-tropical migratory songbirds, raptors, mammals, reptiles and amphibians, and numerous fish species. Bald eagles frequently use refuge habitats for foraging and nesting. Both freshwater and saltwater species are supported with the fishery, which varies with the seasons and accompanying shifts in salinity. The refuge wetlands are important spawning, nursery, and feeding grounds for many aquatic species, including crustaceans and fish species.

Historically, the freshwater marsh within Mandalay NWR has served as important wintering habitat for migratory bird populations. Huge concentrations of waterfowl have wintered in this vicinity in the past. Though marsh conditions have changed and deteriorated due to coastal erosion and saltwater intrusion, this freshwater marsh continues to play a vital role for wintering migratory birds.

Objective 1.1: Manage and protect migratory bird populations.

Discussion: Mandalay NWR was established to provide wintering habitat for migratory birds. Up to twenty duck species, including blue-winged teal, northern pintails, widgeon, gadwall, mallards, and ring-necked ducks, may be found wintering on Mandalay NWR in any given year. In years past, upwards of 20,000 ducks have used the refuge during the fall and winter. The refuge is also used during winter months by white-fronted geese.

Mandalay NWR plans to manage freshwater marsh areas to attain the best quality wintering habitat for migratory bird populations. Mandalay NWR management practices will provide ample submerged and emergent aquatic vegetation as a winter food source for waterfowl. In order to attain the best habitat for wintering waterfowl and promote beneficial native aquatic plant species, the control of invasive/exotic aquatic plant species is critical.

Wading bird rookery areas will be maintained in wooded swamp areas.

Mandalay NWR is home to one active bald eagle nest. Since 2001, the breeding bald eagle pair has fledged 2 young per year, with the exception of 2007 when only 1 fledged.

Shallow water mud flats are important foraging sites for shorebirds. Mandalay NWR is moderately tidally influenced and water levels are drastically influenced from northern fronts during the winter months. During these frontal passages, mud flats are exposed in several areas of shallow marsh. These areas provide for foraging sites for numerous shorebird species including black-necked stilts, dowitchers, yellowlegs, plovers, and sandpipers. For shorebirds, Mandalay NWR and surrounding areas provide important shallow water and mudflat habitat, particularly during the critical fall migration periods. Maintenance of these conditions is critical to the continued use of the area by this group of migratory birds.

Marsh birds use portions of Mandalay NWR year-round. Species such as purple gallinules, common moorhens, least bitterns, American bitterns, and rails are found using areas of freshwater marsh. Marsh birds depend on the erect emergent, herbaceous vegetation and intermingled mud flats for cover, forage, and nests. Pied-billed grebes, gallinules, moorhens, and coots use the open water aquatic beds for foraging. Maintenance of suitable habitat is important to support large numbers of these species.

Usage of the refuge by gulls and terns is thought to be minimal and restricted to foraging. Priority species possibly occurring on the refuge are gull-billed tern (*Sterna nilotica*), and Forester's tern (*Sterna forsteri*).

The location of Mandalay NWR makes it one of the first and last land forms available to trans-Gulf migratory songbirds. The "fingers" of forestland that protrude into the marshes are important for trans-Gulf migratory birds as they gather the nutrient reserves in preparation for or recovery from trans-Gulf migration. Management to maintain and possibly enhance or expand the area of forested wetlands on the refuge is encouraged. These areas are also important nesting sites for prothonotary warblers (*Protonotaria citrea*).

Strategies:

- Maintain wood duck boxes.
- Survey migratory wintering waterfowl and other species such as mottled ducks and black bellied whistling ducks to determine and record trends in waterfowl distribution.
- Band wood ducks, mottled ducks, and black bellied whistling ducks when the opportunity arises.
- Establish a partnership between the refuge and the research community to promote monitoring and researching to determine the most effective methods for waterfowl management.
- Modify management actions to improve waterfowl and other wildlife habitat.
- Conduct wading bird rookery surveys.
- Conduct bald eagle survey to attain use of refuge and monitor nest site off of Ridge Canal.
- Protect existing cypress stands on Mandalay NWR, located primarily within swamp habitat adjacent to the natural ridge.
- Protect any nesting bald eagles from disturbance that could lead to nest abandonment.
- Conduct marsh bird survey to attain use of marsh and open water habitats.
- Explore possibility of conducting migratory songbird surveys to attain use of marsh and forested wetland areas by non-game migratory songbirds.

Objective 1.2: Manage and protect threatened and endangered species through implementation of recovery plans.

Discussion: Currently, no threatened or endangered species use the refuge year-round. There is no critical threatened and endangered habitat present on the refuge. Only on rare occurrences, the refuge may be used temporarily by these species as they migrate through the area.

Strategy:

- Monitor any subsequent use of the refuge by migrating endangered species.

Objective 1.3: Monitor species of concern, targeted species, and species of federal responsibility in order to assess management goals.

Discussion: American alligators are opportunistic carnivores and a top predator on the refuge. Mandalay NWR participates in the state alligator harvest program every fall. Alligator surveys are conducted on Mandalay NWR, including a spotlight population count by refuge staff and an aerial nest count by LDWF. The annual harvest quota (alligator tag allotment) and season dates are determined by LDWF each year, and are based on several environmental factors including habitat type, annual productivity, and harvest data from previous years.

Mandalay NWR also participates in the coast-wide nutria harvest program coordinated by LDWF. Each year, a minimum quota of nutria assigned to each trapper, set by the refuge staff, is harvested from Mandalay NWR. The nutria is an invasive exotic herbivorous species from South America. It destroys healthy marsh habitats by foraging on marsh vegetation thereby further increasing marsh deterioration and coastal erosion. In some instances, these marsh habitats are so damaged that it may take years for the vegetation to return. This rebound usually occurs only if the nutria population is reduced well below the carrying capacity of these fragile marsh habitats.

Swine are regularly introduced into the wild in Louisiana, creating populations of feral hogs. These hogs are generally live-captured and moved from occupied to unoccupied areas. Feral hogs are prolific, with reproductive rates four times that of native ungulate species. Feral hogs jeopardize the refuge mission by damaging habitat and impacting native plant and animal species. They have been documented to cause soil erosion, leaching of minerals and nutrients, habitat destruction, native plant species destruction, exotic plant species invasion, and changes in vegetative succession rates. Feral hogs also impact native wildlife through direct competition for food and predation of native amphibians, reptiles, mammals and ground-nesting birds.

Strategies:

- Conduct alligator surveys and harvest program (refer to Mandalay NWR alligator and furbearer plan).
- Continue to participate in the nutria control program (refer to Mandalay NWR alligator and furbearer plan).
- Continue feral hog control (refer to Mandalay NWR hunt plan).

Objective 1.4: Monitor resident and other species utilizing habitat on the refuge.

Discussion: The refuge currently supports a population of white-tailed deer (*Odocoileus virginianus*) that appears to be of relatively low density. The habitat on the refuge is not consistent with quality deer habitat due to low elevations and year-round inundation. There are areas of higher elevation on the refuge that include forested habitat and provide better management opportunities for game animals. These areas occur mostly on spoil banks and on the wooded ridge in that portion of the refuge south of the Gulf Intracoastal Waterway. These forested areas include hard-mast bearing trees and other woody species beneficial to deer and other small mammals. Deer use the marsh areas for foraging on herbaceous vegetation, but management options for those habitats are limited.

Squirrels (*Sciurus carolinensis*) and rabbits (*Sylvilagus aquaticus*) are the two primary small game animals on the refuge. The above-mentioned forest management practices would improve squirrel habitat. Squirrels are cavity nesters and any forest management plan developed for the refuge should contain some protection of cavity trees for squirrel den sites in addition to promoting hard-mast producing trees.

The rabbit population on the refuge is subject to seasonal fluctuations due to the hydrology of the area. Most of the refuge is flooded year-round and the remaining areas flood occasionally either from high water levels in the Atchafalaya River or from strong southerly winds pushing water up from the Gulf. These unpredictable high-water events can dramatically impact the rabbit population, particularly when they occur during the spring when the rabbits are nesting. Rabbit populations tend to recover quickly without any additional management.

Coastal Louisiana traditionally supports a significant population of furbearers including raccoon, otter, muskrat, mink and bobcat. Since nutria have become established in the region, native aquatic furbearer populations have declined. Controlling the nutria population is by far the most proactive management strategy that benefits the native aquatic furbearers on the refuge.

Strategies:

- Conduct forage surveys for white-tailed deer, herd density (browse surveys), and monitor harvest.
- Explore possibility of surveys for squirrel and rabbit abundance.
- Survey densities of other fur-bearer species using habitat on the refuge.

Objective 1.5: Monitor fish and shellfish habitat on the refuge.

Discussion: The marshes on the upper end of the Bayou Penchant estuary provide nursery grounds for many fish and shellfish found in the Gulf of Mexico, including white shrimp, brown shrimp, blue crab, Gulf menhaden, Atlantic croaker, bay anchovy, spot and Atlantic threadfin. Freshwater sportfishing for largemouth bass, crappie, sunfish, and catfish is popular and commercial fishers catch catfish and gar within the surrounding vicinity of the refuge. Salinity can rise in the waters of Mandalay NWR following significant weather patterns. Most recently (2005), Hurricane Rita raised marsh salinities to 8-10ppm. Decaying storm debris increased oxygen demand and caused significant fish kills in the area.

Strategies:

- Monitor fish and shellfish species present on refuge via coordination with LDWF's Wildlife and Fisheries Inland and Marine Fish Divisions and report all fish kills.
- Continue correspondence with local fishermen and sportsmen to assess species in daily catch.

GOAL 2. To restore, improve, and maintain a mosaic of wetland habitats native to the Terrebonne Basin in order to ensure healthy and viable plant and animal communities, with an emphasis on migratory bird species.

Background: The key purpose of the refuge is to provide habitat for a natural diversity of wildlife, with emphasis on wintering and nesting habitat for migratory and resident waterfowl, non-game migratory birds, and threatened and endangered species.

Mandalay NWR is in the Terrebonne Basin. From 1978-1990, 61 percent of all coastal land loss occurred within the Terrebonne and Barataria Basins when compared to the seven remaining Louisiana coastal hydrologic basins defined by the CWPPRA Task Force. Most of the Terrebonne Basin losses were interior marshes with some non-fresh land losses skirting the bays (Barras et al. 1994).

Additionally, the USGS has documented approximately 19 sq mi (49 sq km) of land lost from October 2004 to October 2005 in the Terrebonne Basin following Hurricanes Katrina and Rita (Barras 2006).

The refuge has experienced land losses from both internal marsh break-up as well as considerable shoreline erosion along the Gulf Intracoastal Waterway. From 1944 to 1983, the north and south shorelines of the waterway in the vicinity of Mandalay NWR have experienced an average land loss rate of approximately 13.17 ft/yr (May and Britsch 1987).

In 2003, the Mandalay Bank Protection Demonstration CWPPRA project (TE-41) was constructed along the southern shoreline of the Gulf Intracoastal Waterway. This 5-year demonstration project is intended to evaluate several structural erosion control treatments in the highly organic soils along the waterway in the refuge (Segura 2001) for potentially less-costly erosion control techniques. Monitoring is on-going and it is too early at this time to form conclusions (Lear and Dearmond 2005).

Objective 2.1: Manage, maintain, and improve when possible fresh and intermediate marsh and other aquatic habitats for refuge resources.

Discussion: The refuge features freshwater marshes intersected by a major ridge with associated swamp borders. It contains freshwater marshes (approximately 3,500ac) that are diverse and nutrient rich habitats which play a vital role in the hydrology of this region and are home to an abundance of fish and wildlife species. The marsh soils are primarily organic and mucky, and are affected by some sediment recharge from the lower Atchafalaya River. Drainage is south to the Gulf of Mexico.

Strategies:

- Monitor impacts of public use on habitat.
- Control invasive plant species and invasive exotic mammals (refer to Mandalay Hunt Plan and Furbearer Trapping Plan)
- Erosion control along the Gulf Intracoastal Waterway and other shorelines, placement of hard structures along the waterway, and restoration of the waterway bank line.
- Maintain lakes and ponds.
- Maintain and increase production of fish and wildlife species when possible.
- Creation of flotant marsh via cooperation with research projects, state and federal agencies, and coastal restoration grants.
- Structural hydrologic management via completion of proposed Hanson Unit Marsh project and replacement of water control structure on Ridge Canal.
- Continuously maintain marsh restoration and management project proposals on file and search for funding sources/partners to assist in implementation, and seek new funding for future enhancement projects.
- Develop a habitat management plan by 2013.

Objective 2.2: Manage, maintain, and enhance when possible bottomland hardwood and cypress/tupelo swamp habitats and associated ridges and spoil banks for refuge resources.

Discussion: The refuge contains approximately 50 acres of bordering swamps, 175 acres of upland ridges, and approximately 800 acres of oil field canals and other bodies of water. The cypress/tupelo swamp areas provide excellent rookery habitat for wading birds and play an important role in the hydrology of the refuge. The ridge soils are Sharkey clay in nature, and the narrow ridge is farmed for sugarcane to the north of the refuge. The north and south portion of the ridge is bisected by the Gulf Intracoastal Waterway. The portion of the ridge on the refuge is bisected by an oil field location canal. This ridge and associated spoil banks along the canals contain several large hard mast tree species and an abundance of soft mast species. The ridge and associated spoil banks provide protection to interior marsh from erosion factors of the waterway, primarily wave action from large marine transportation vessels.

Strategies:

- Stabilize shorelines via cooperation with research projects, state and federal agencies, and coastal restoration grants.
- Plant hardwood species when opportunity arises.
- Develop a habitat management plan by 2013.

Objective 2.3: Support partnerships to protect natural habitats of the Terrebonne Basin.

Discussion: Since the establishment of Mandalay NWR, there has been a cooperative agreement with Terrebonne Parish to support coastal restoration efforts along the Gulf Intracoastal Waterway and portions of marsh within the refuge. Christmas tree cradles were established along the north bank of the waterway to prevent erosion. Also, several marsh grass plantings have occurred within the south end of the Hanson Unit over the last several years through coordination with Terrebonne Parish and the Natural Resources Conservation Service. These grass plantings have been an overall success by diverting wave action from the waterway and minimizing the passage of aquatic invasive species into the interior marsh of the Hanson Unit.

Strategies:

- Continue cooperation with Terrebonne Parish and Natural Resources Conservation Service with marsh grass plantings and Christmas tree cradles on the refuge.
- Continue to cooperate with LDNR and the TE41 bank stabilization project on the refuge.
- Promote grass planting efforts to local community and school groups.

Goal 3. Provide opportunities for wildlife-dependent recreation and environmental education and interpretation in accordance with the Improvement Act.

Background: Mandalay NWR is a relatively young refuge (established 1996). Management efforts during the first 10 years have been focused on the following priorities: maintenance of migratory bird habitat; exotic/invasive plant and animal control; and public use and wildlife-dependent recreation. The refuge was opened to public use in 2000, and currently hosts hunting, fishing, and wildlife observation activities. Public hunting opportunities include archery deer and hog, lottery youth and adult waterfowl, and recreational fishing. Additionally, alligator and nutria are harvested under special use management permits.

Fishing is the most common form of public use on the refuge. Fishing for largemouth bass, bream, and catfish is very popular with local fishermen. Sport fishing in this region is considered to be a traditional form of wildlife-dependent recreation. Refuge regulations against unsupervised lines and nets and night activities have restricted pre-establishment activities of frogging, trotlines, jug lines, and nets. Current fishing is restricted to recreational hook and line fishing from boats and banks.

The Mandalay Nature Trail provides public recreational opportunities via hiking, wildlife observation, wildlife photography, and environmental education and interpretation.

Objective 3.1: Develop and implement a Visitor Services Management Plan

Discussion: A visitor services plan is critical to the future direction of the refuge's visitor services program. This plan will communicate the goals, objectives, and strategies for the visitor services program and will outline future funding and staffing needs. The plan will also demonstrate how the visitor services program is integrated with the natural and cultural resources management program and supports visitor understanding and appreciation of the natural and cultural resources of the refuge.

The majority of Mandalay NWR is accessible by boat only; in March 2007, a nature trail near the headquarters was opened. This strip of property runs through bottomland hardwoods into a fresh marsh area. It provides vehicle access to a portion of the refuge. A visitor contact station is located within the headquarters building. The majority of visitors are recreational fishermen or hunters, but since the nature trail has opened there has been an increase in visits for wildlife observation and photography.

Strategy:

- Develop a Visitor Services Management Plan by 2015.

Objective 3.2: Provide opportunities for hunting and fishing on the refuge in a manner which minimizes conflicts between consumptive and non-consumptive user groups.

Discussion: Hunting and fishing have been identified as priority public uses of the Refuge System. Where appropriate and compatible, the best hunting and fishing opportunities possible will be made available to the public. Historically, this area of south Louisiana is well known for its hunting, fishing, and trapping traditions. These wildlife-dependent practices are ingrained in the culture of south Louisiana. The continuation of these hunting and fishing activities is very important to the local community as Mandalay NWR is one of the few public areas accessible to the public. The majority of land surrounding the refuge is owned by large corporations or families and lease prices for these properties are increasing year-by-year. The refuge supplies the locals with an area to hunt and fish, as long as they abide by the rules and regulations of the refuge. Through harvest of these natural renewable resources, the refuge staff is able to manage and maintain wildlife populations at carrying capacity and maintain the integrity of the habitat.

Strategies:

- Evaluate user groups on a yearly basis.
- Maintain harvest records and make evaluations of harvest on a yearly basis.
- Manage hunting and fishing programs to achieve population management and wildlife habitat objectives.

Objective 3.3: Provide opportunities for wildlife observation and wildlife photography on the refuge.

Discussion: Wildlife observation and wildlife photography are two closely related priority wildlife-dependent recreational uses of the Refuge System. Programs and facilities which enable visitors to view and photograph wildlife and their habitats are an essential part of most national wildlife refuges. The Mandalay Nature Trail provides the public with easy access to the refuge for wildlife observation and wildlife photography, especially for tourists visiting Terrebonne Parish. However, some of the most beautiful areas of the refuge are accessed by boat. Local swamp tours provide visitors insight into the expansive freshwater marshes and cypress/tupelo swamps near the refuge. Because of the tremendous volumes of water in Terrebonne Parish, many of the locals have a boat or access to a vessel. Many of our hunters and fishermen also enjoy wildlife observation while utilizing the refuge.

Strategies:

- Maintain and improve the Mandalay Nature Trail for birding and interpretation.
- Maintain habitat on the refuge and maintain access points for watercraft where applicable.

Objective 3.4: Increase public outreach to emphasize resource management practices.

Discussion: The staff presently participates in 6-8 events each year. These events include local festivals and community group meetings, and the Wildthings Festival in Lacombe. Currently, Mandalay NWR has no visitor services staff. Plans to participate in any additional activities with current staff are not feasible.

Strategy:

- Continue current programs with minimal staffing; if staffing increases, provide more outreach services.

Objective 3.5: Provide interpretation that promotes understanding, appreciation, and stewardship of refuge resources.

Discussion: The Mandalay NWR headquarters currently provides a visitor contact station. In the future, with ample space available at the headquarters, a visitor information and interpretive center will be designed and constructed within the headquarters building. In the near future, provide information panels for the 3 newly constructed kiosks.

Strategy:

- Improve office visitor contact area and develop interpretive panels for office and on Mandalay Nature Trail.

Objective 3.6: Provide environmental education programs that promote understanding, appreciation, and stewardship of refuge resources.

Discussion: Emphasis will be placed on the unique habitats within the refuge, the wetland forests, and freshwater marshes. Programs and opportunities will be designed to enhance public awareness of coastal erosion issues, to restore wetland areas, and to increase environmental stewardship. The staff usually hosts several visits a year from local community groups such as Boy Scout troops, garden club, bird club, and school groups. Staff members usually makes time in their schedule to accommodate these activities. Currently, the refuge has no education/outreach staff.

Strategy:

- Develop environmental education program on refuge and in local schools if staffing increases.

Objective 3.7: Manage the volunteer program to enhance all aspects of refuge management.

Discussion: The refuge has a handful of volunteers that assist with mostly maintenance projects. Staff will continue to coordinate with these volunteers to accomplish projects on the refuge when funding for such projects become available.

Strategies:

- Maintain relationship with local Terrebonne Parish bird club, local garden club, and local volunteers.
- Develop a friends group when additional staff is added to administer support.

GOAL 4. Protect the natural and cultural resources of the refuge to ensure their integrity and to fulfill the mission of the Refuge System.

Background: Inherent in ensuring that future generations can enjoy the refuge is protection of its resources. Cultural resources include archaeological resources, historic and architectural properties, and areas or sites of tradition or religious significance to Native Americans (614 FW 1, Policy, Responsibilities and Definitions). No comprehensive survey of refuge cultural resources has been completed, but local archaeologists and refuge staff have knowledge of several Native American middens (e.g., refuse piles) located along drainages off the refuge. Enforcement of laws pertaining to wildlife and other natural resources is fundamental and necessary, especially in areas of high public use. The safety and protection of the people using the refuge is a priority. Also considered in this goal is protection of the resources by acquisition of land included in the approved acquisition boundary.

Objective 4.1: Protect known archaeological and historical sites on the refuge from illegal take or damage in compliance with the Archaeological Resources Protections Act, the Native American Graves Protection and Repatriation Act, and the National Historic Preservation Act.

Discussion: Although no thorough survey of the entire refuge has been accomplished, middens are known to exist on banks of bayous just south of the refuge. These are obviously places where nomadic groups camped as evidenced by mounds of clam shells left in the refuse piles. The slightly higher elevation of the middens often create habitat for live oak trees.

Strategies:

- Maintain refuge lands intact by preventing destruction or disturbance of historical ridge sites within the refuge.
- Contact local and national archaeological groups and cultural groups to determine if any management activities may impact their archaeological sites.

Objective 4.2: Maintain marked refuge boundary and other identifying/directional signs.

Discussion: Mandalay NWR is a relatively new refuge within the Refuge System, and is still being surveyed to determine refuge boundaries. The majority of the boundary is posted, yet some of these areas are affected by high water moving aquatic vegetation over the boundary posts, and in some cases the posts are lost in the marsh. Because of frequent storm damage and vandalism, sign replacement is necessary. Therefore, refuge boundary signing is of high priority. Direction and informational signs should be written in clear, concise language and placed in appropriate locations.

Strategies:

- Maintain boundary signs and refuge entrance signs.
- Within 10 years of the date of this CCP, evaluate all refuge signage and replace/add signs as needed

Objective 4.3: Provide for visitor safety, protect resources, and ensure the public's compliance with refuge regulations.

Discussion: Public uses are limited to those that are compatible with refuge purposes, realizing that wildlife needs and requirements come first. Therefore, protection of wildlife resources and laws pertaining to wildlife are a priority of refuge law enforcement. Because of moderate visitor use, law enforcement personnel also deal with issues such as hunter safety, illegal drugs, vandalism, thefts, littering, and safety of visitors. Visitors should be able to enjoy a pleasurable experience with adequate and safe access.

Strategies:

- Hire a full-time law enforcement officer.
- Retain co-lateral duty officer currently on staff.
- Work cooperatively with local, state, and other federal law enforcement agencies to enhance resource protection.

Objective 4.4: Acquire those lands identified in the approved acquisition boundary.

Discussion: The 1996 establishing documents of Mandalay NWR contain an approved acquisition boundary. Because of the severity of coastal erosion and importance of freshwater marsh habitat in south Louisiana, lands should be acquired by the Service that fall within the Mandalay NWR acquisition boundary.

Strategy:

- When funding becomes available, purchase lands from willing sellers within the acquisition boundary.

Objective 4.5: Maintain more than $3,000,000 worth of capitalized equipment for the complex of eight refuges to be used in all aspects of refuge administration, including habitat, wildlife, public use, and protection projects and management.

Discussion: The majority of equipment used by the Mandalay NWR staff is excess equipment acquired from other refuges and government agencies. Since Mandalay NWR is one of a complex of eight refuges, equipment is shared among the refuges instead of being assigned solely to Mandalay NWR. The equipment referred to here is not separate from the other refuges in the Complex. Project efficiency depends largely on age, condition, and maintenance of the equipment needed to accomplish work projects.

Strategies:

- Maintain programs, personnel, and equipment.
- Maintain a current data base containing all capitalized equipment and a maintenance. schedule. Hire staff maintenance person to maintain equipment and facilities.
- Replace or purchase additional equipment as needed in order to have well-maintained and working equipment for all force account work planned.

V. Plan Implementation

INTRODUCTION

Refuge lands are managed as defined under the Improvement Act. Congress has distinguished a clear legislative mission of wildlife conservation for all national wildlife refuges. National wildlife refuges, unlike other public lands, are dedicated to the conservation of the Nation's fish and wildlife resources and wildlife-dependent recreational uses. Priority projects emphasize the protection and enhancement of fish and wildlife species first and foremost, but considerable emphasis is placed on balancing the needs and demands for wildlife-dependent recreation and environmental education.

To accomplish the purpose, vision, goals, and objectives contained in this CCP, this section identifies projects, funding and personnel needs, volunteers, partnerships opportunities, step-down management plans, a monitoring and adaptive management plan, and plan review and revision.

This CCP focuses on the importance of funding the operations and maintenance needs of the refuge to ensure the staff can achieve the goals and objectives identified and are crucial to fulfill the purpose for which the refuge was established. The refuge's role in protecting and providing habitat for waterfowl and endangered species is important. Proposed priority public use programs will establish and expand opportunities for wildlife-dependent recreation, but not without adequate resources.

The following projects reflect basic needs of the refuge as identified during the development of this CCP.

PROPOSED PROJECTS

Listed below are the proposed project summaries and their associated costs for fish and wildlife population management, habitat management, resource protection, visitor services, and refuge administration over the next 15 years. This proposed project list reflects the priority needs identified by the public, planning team, and refuge staff based upon available information. These projects were generated for the purpose of achieving the refuge's objectives and strategies. The primary linkages of these projects to those planning elements are identified in each summary.

FISH AND WILDLIFE POPULATION MANAGEMENT

The refuge attracts 18 species of waterfowl, of which the mottled duck, wood duck, and black-bellied whistling duck nest on the refuge. Over 20,000 waterfowl have been documented to use the refuge for resting and feeding during peak migrations. Shorebirds, marsh birds, wading birds, neotropical migratory songbirds, raptors including osprey, mammals, reptiles and amphibians, and numerous fisheries exist on the refuge. Bald eagles also inhabit the refuge by utilizing habitat for foraging and nesting. The refuge marsh wetlands are spawning, nursery, and feeding grounds for many aquatic species.

Freshwater species are supported with the fishery varying with the seasons and accompanying shifts in salinity. The refuge wetlands are important spawning, nursery, and feeding grounds for many aquatic species, including crustaceans and fish species. On occasion, when salinities increase, saltwater species may use the refuge.

Project 1 – Monitor waterfowl use on refuge.

Hunting is offered on a portion of the refuge two days a week until noon during the State of Louisiana State Waterfowl Season. A large portion of the refuge area remains closed to waterfowl hunting. This provides "safe" habitat for resting and feeding to thousands of migratory waterfowl without hunting pressure. Refuge staff will monitor migrating and wintering waterfowl use.

- Conduct annual waterfowl aerial surveys consisting of four to six surveys contingent on weather conditions. Initial survey will be performed before state waterfowl hunting season begins and last survey will be conducted after state waterfowl hunting season ends.
- Coordinate with LDWF on migration numbers on refuge.

Two biologists will be required to conduct surveys on the refuge. The annual cost will be $2,000.

Project 2 – Monitor species of concern, targeted species, and species of federal responsibility.

National wildlife refuges are mandated to manage for threatened and endangered species if they occur on the refuge. However, refuges are also responsible for management of all native species if the action does not negatively impact the threatened or endangered species. Refuge management is geared toward managing the ecosystem as a whole.

- An overall faunal species list will be compiled from surveys conducted by Service and other researchers. This list will be made available to the public through the refuge website. Within the list, refuge staff will prioritize species based on regional and state lists of species of concern, at risk/target species identified by Partners in Flight, and other plans.
- Develop a wildlife inventory plan based on species selected as priority species.
- Annual waterfowl surveys will be conducted from October to February.
- Secretive marsh birds will be surveyed and monitored as species of concern. Adaptive refuge management actions will reflect data collected.

Project 3 – Provide brood habitat and nest sites for wood ducks to support 200 hatching wood ducks each year.

The wood duck population increase is a success story resulting from the introduction of the wood duck box nest program. They are a common resident in freshwater swamps, sloughs, and marshes. Wood ducks seek tree cavities within 1 mile of water. However, brood success is significantly higher when nests are next to water. Forested wetlands, scrub/shrub areas, and tree lined bayous, canals, and sloughs are the preferred habitats of nesting wood ducks.

- The refuge will install and annually maintain 30 wood duck boxes in hardwood sloughs, swamps, and marsh edges throughout the refuge.

Wood duck nesting cavities and habitat are abundant on the refuge and within the surrounding area. As a result, nest box usage has been minimal in past years. Maintenance costs of $5,000 are needed annually to maintain this program.

HABITAT MANAGEMENT

The refuge provides a diversity of habitats for resident and migratory faunal species, including wetland, aquatic, forestland, and scrub/shrub habitats. The purposes for which the refuge was established include providing natural habitat for wintering and nesting waterfowl, non-game birds, and threatened and endangered species.

Project 1 – Restore marsh in open pond areas over 5 acres in size and fortify the shoreline of the refuge to ensure healthy and viable plant and animal communities and protect the integrity of the refuge habitats.

The reduction or attempted halt of marsh subsidence and marsh loss is considered critical through marsh creation projects and plantings for marsh stabilization.

- Develop grants through NAWCA, CWPPRA, and partnerships with the Barataria-Terrebonne National Estuary Program, The Nature Conservancy, local universities, and other organizations to restore marsh habitats in open water ponds to encourage less than 5-acre pond sizes and resulting increased emergent marsh.
- Develop terracing, Christmas tree structures, dedicated dredging projects, etc., to accomplish this objective.
- Utilize proven techniques for shoreline stabilization.
- Once new lands are formed, plant desired marsh grass if necessary.

Project 2 – Use beneficial dredged materials from the Gulf Intracoastal Waterway, through cooperation with the Army Corps of Engineers (Corps) when applicable, to fill open water areas and create new emergent marsh on the refuge. These actions can create and restore hundreds of acres lost to erosion and subsidence on the refuge with little to no costs to the refuge.

- Partner with the Corps to plan location and elevation of material to be stacked on refuge.
- Plan locations of sediment to ensure that tidal movement will reach all areas. No areas of stagnated water shall exist.
- Monitor areas for vegetation growth and inventory species.
- Once new lands are formed, plant desired marsh grass if necessary.
- Identify wildlife use and monitor their use of the new area.

The cost for sediment placement will vary, but the funds will be through the Corps navigation projects and should be no immediate cost to the refuge. The inventory of plants and wildlife can be accomplished by one biologist for $5,000 annually. Planting can be accomplished using volunteers and a one-time cost of $40,000 for plants, travel, and supplies.

The reduction or attempted halt of marsh subsidence and marsh loss is considered critical through marsh creation projects and plantings for marsh stabilization.

Project 3 – Develop monitoring programs for marsh loss, change in water depths, submerged aquatic plants, and the impacts of public use activities on the resources. Evaluate long-term effects of restoration and shoreline fortification projects.

- Develop historic GIS maps of soils, habitats, and boundaries.
- Establish salinity monitoring points and monitor monthly by taking readings, developing a spreadsheet database, and evaluating changes. Coordinate with marsh survivability plots and vegetation composition changes.
- Map vegetation types with the use of GPS and GIS to inventory special and unique areas of the refuge requiring special management or protection.
- Implement a marsh subsidence monitoring plan to monitor the effects of refuge habitat manipulations and the encouragement of wildlife plants, such as three-square and duck potato in the marsh. These plans will show impacts of higher salinity to freshwater marsh resources and impacts to resources for wildlife on the refuge.

Operational funds should be dedicated for trained personnel performing basic wildlife inventorying and monitoring. One biologist and one technician are needed to perform inventorying, monitoring, and managing restoration and management programs. Sampling schemes will use photo points and transects to monitor changes from management actions. These monitoring programs will employ the use of field computers, data collectors, boats, and GIS technology for documentation. A cost estimate per year of $30,000 will be required for this work to be achieved. This is primarily salary costs.

RESOURCE PROTECTION AND REFUGE ADMINISTRATION

Project 1 – Provide adequate law enforcement protection for refuge resources, federal trust species, personnel, and the visiting public.

Mandalay NWR hosts approximately 20,000 visitors annually for hunting, fishing, and other wildlife-dependent recreation. The refuge will conduct a refuge law enforcement program review and revise the law enforcement plan. One full-time law enforcement position is needed and can patrol both Mandalay and Bayou Teche NWRs to cooperate with state wildlife officers and the local sheriff and city officers to:

- Protect hunters, fishermen, and other visitors and otherwise provide a safe experience while they are on the refuge.
- Enforce refuge regulations and reduce unapproved and illegal activities.
- Rescue lost or stranded hunters, fishermen, and aid visitors in need.
- Protect refuge infrastructure, equipment, and cultural and natural resources.
- Conduct patrols in refuge owned waterways or ponds for illegal commercial fishing activities.

One refuge officer is needed to achieve goals and perform law enforcement duties. Cost would be $90,000 per year for salary, equipment, and supplies.

Project 2 – Maintain marked refuge boundary and other identifying and regulating signs.

- Conduct refuge boundary surveys on all lands and any new lands when acquired and post accordingly.
- All existing refuge boundaries will be inspected and reposted by annually inspecting and reposting 20 percent of the refuge boundary.
- Signs will be placed at all refuge entrance points along trails, water courses, and roads.
- Post signs to mark the portions of the refuge as "closed" so they are visible at all entrances.
- Replace all faded or damaged signs as observed.

The one-time cost for boundary surveys will be $20,000 due to logistics. The annual boundary maintenance cost will be $5,000.

Project 3 – Meet current and expanded ability to maintain infrastructure for public use and management capabilities of the refuge.

A maintenance and field headquarters is located in Houma. There are two employees stationed there but no maintenance employee. All other employees are stationed at the Southeast Louisiana NWR Complex in Lacombe.

- Staff share responsibilities with other refuges. Equipment, office space, roads, parking areas, refuge facilities, boats, and vehicles must be maintained regularly through a maintenance management system. There is a need for one maintenance staff for upkeep of facilities and equipment.

Project 4 – Administer oil and gas program with efforts guided to protect surface habitat and wildlife on the refuge.

Mandalay NWR has one active gas well and collection facility located on the Sunrise Canal. There are numerous plugged and abandoned wells throughout the refuge. Seven major transmission pipelines (8 miles) traverse the refuge. Spill events and releases are rare occurrences on the refuge. All activities relating to oil and gas on the refuge must be requested through a special use permit for review.

- Ensure all companies operating on refuge are permitted, identified, and in compliance with refuge, state, and industry regulations.
- All activities are submitted for review and a determination is made by refuge manager if a special use permit is required for activities requested or performed.
- Issue special use permits and assess mitigation for impacts to the surface of the refuge if they cannot be avoided.
- Response to all spill events and releases are conducted immediately after located; however, before work is performed, the response/clean-up company must consult with the refuge manager to ensure methods are approved on refuge.
- Conduct routine inspections of field and facility to ensure proper operating procedures are in place and no releases are occurring.
- Provide guidance for wildlife oriented protection methods such as bird cannons, steamers, and predator eyes during spill events.

Project 5 – Acquire lands identified within the approved acquisition boundary.

- Acquire lands from willing sellers with the assistance of the Service's Realty Office.
- Prioritize land acquisitions by tract numbers or names to areas under the most threat to the natural resources.
- Determine if any acquired lands deserve inclusion in the wilderness system through a wilderness review.

VISITOR SERVICES

Access to Mandalay NWR is primarily by boat only, except for the nature trail. The area is known across southeast Louisiana as a premier fishing destination that will continue to draw visitors locally and from out of the State of Louisiana for opportunities for outdoor recreation.

Project 1 – Maintain facilities at the Mandalay NWR office.

The office has established a large kiosk that offers information about the Service and the refuge, wildlife, other brochures, and hunting permits.

- Maintenance of facilities and all equipment located on-site is performed by a 2-person staff stationed in Houma and a part-time law enforcement officer stationed in Franklin.

An assistant refuge manager is needed in Houma. The cost will be $90,000 per year for salary, benefits, equipment, and supplies.

Project 2 – Improve visitor services and interpretation.

Established in 1996, Mandalay NWR has never been fully developed to the potential of programs, facilities, and staff to best support visitor services and wildlife-dependent recreation.

One of the first and primary duties is to develop a step-down Visitor Services Plan with services that include wildlife-dependent recreation and education. Refuge staff will:

- Update Visitor Services Plan.
- Post visitor hours and contact information and maintain a staff contact presence throughout those hours (by phone at minimum).
- Staff will develop, maintain, and improve interpretive exhibits for the new kiosk and develop interpretive talks specific to each refuge.
- Volunteers will be used to supplement the education programs and visitor contact centers.
- Improve visitor contact stations, nature trail, kiosks, parking areas, and maintain refuge entrance sign quality and appearance.

Project 3 – Improve and enhance hunting and fishing opportunities while minimizing conflicts between consumptive and non-consumptive users.

Quality fishing opportunities may be promoted with initiatives. Fishing opportunities at Mandalay NWR have been minimal and only opportunistic. The refuge staff will provide:

- Maintain kiosks at the Mandalay NWR Office, local public boat launch, and at the nature trail to promote safe hunting and fishing opportunities.
- Provide hunting and fishing brochures with maps.
- Continue hunting program for big game and waterfowl.

Project 4 – Provide opportunities for wildlife observation and photography.

Wildlife observation and photography opportunities on the refuges will be promoted. Mandalay NWR provides emergent marsh habitats for viewing waterfowl, shorebirds, wading birds, and a variety of other fauna and flora.

- Offer occasional birding tours led by refuge staff or volunteers.
- Provide temporary photo blinds in designated areas by staff.
- Provide a viewing area at nature trail with interpretive panels and benches.
- Develop a self-guided boat tour with information guiding visitors as to what they might expect to see depending on the time of year.

Project 5 – Increase public outreach and environmental education to emphasize resource management practices.

Marsh restoration and other refuge habitat management programs can be a source of information for educating the public about refuge resources and management. Education on refuge management will be focused on first-hand observations where possible. Interpretation of refuge resources will promote understanding, appreciation, and stewardship of refuge resources.

- Develop a formal, curriculum-based environmental education program for students in Terrebonne Parish and surrounding parishes that, through first-hand experiences, promote understanding, appreciation, and stewardship of refuge resources and support for refuge management practices. Small group tours can be achieved when properly planned.
- To complement on-site programming, provide relevant classroom educational programming with the same goals of promoting understanding and stewardship of refuge resources.
- Establish schedule of tours available for refuge visitors.
- Develop general brochures of the refuges and distribute.
- Supply refuge brochures, including hunt brochures, bird lists, general brochures, and quarterly events calendars, to parish convention centers, state welcome centers, and other tourist hubs.
- Provide schedules of planned programs to local newspapers and use volunteers, members of local bird groups, interns, and refuge staff.
- Establish times at the facility office to have environmental education programs available for the public or groups upon request. Provide guided outings schedules to local newspapers.
- Recruit full-time volunteer interns to supplement refuge staff in delivering school curriculum-based environmental education programs, refuge interpretive programs, and to assist refuge personnel in refuge management, while providing developmental experiences that allow students to explore future career opportunities with the Service.
- Recruit volunteers and volunteer groups, such as recreational vehicle campers, to supplement and assist refuge staff, and to provide education, visitor services, maintenance, and clerical duties.
- Issue press releases on important events on the refuge, including public events and changes to public use programs (e.g., hunting and fishing).
- Update and maintain an interactive refuge web site with links to hunt brochures, bird lists, trail maps and guides, refuge maps, tear sheets, contacts for refuge assistance, signup for programs, etc.
- Develop and deliver refuge education programs for adults through civic groups and to neighborhood groups surrounding the refuge.
- Develop portion of office in Houma to a visitor center, featuring information on visitor service opportunities on the refuge, audio-visual interpretive exhibits and displays, and environmental education resources for visiting school groups and teachers.

FUNDING AND PERSONNEL

The current refuge complex staffing chart includes staff identified for both Mandalay and Bayou Teche NWRs (Figure 7). The proposed staffing chart (Figure 8) will utilize identified staff to accomplish the proposed projects (Table 1).

Figure 7. Current staffing chart for Mandalay and Bayou Teche National Wildlife Refuges

Southeast Louisiana National Wildlife Refuges
Lacombe, LA

Current Organizational Chart

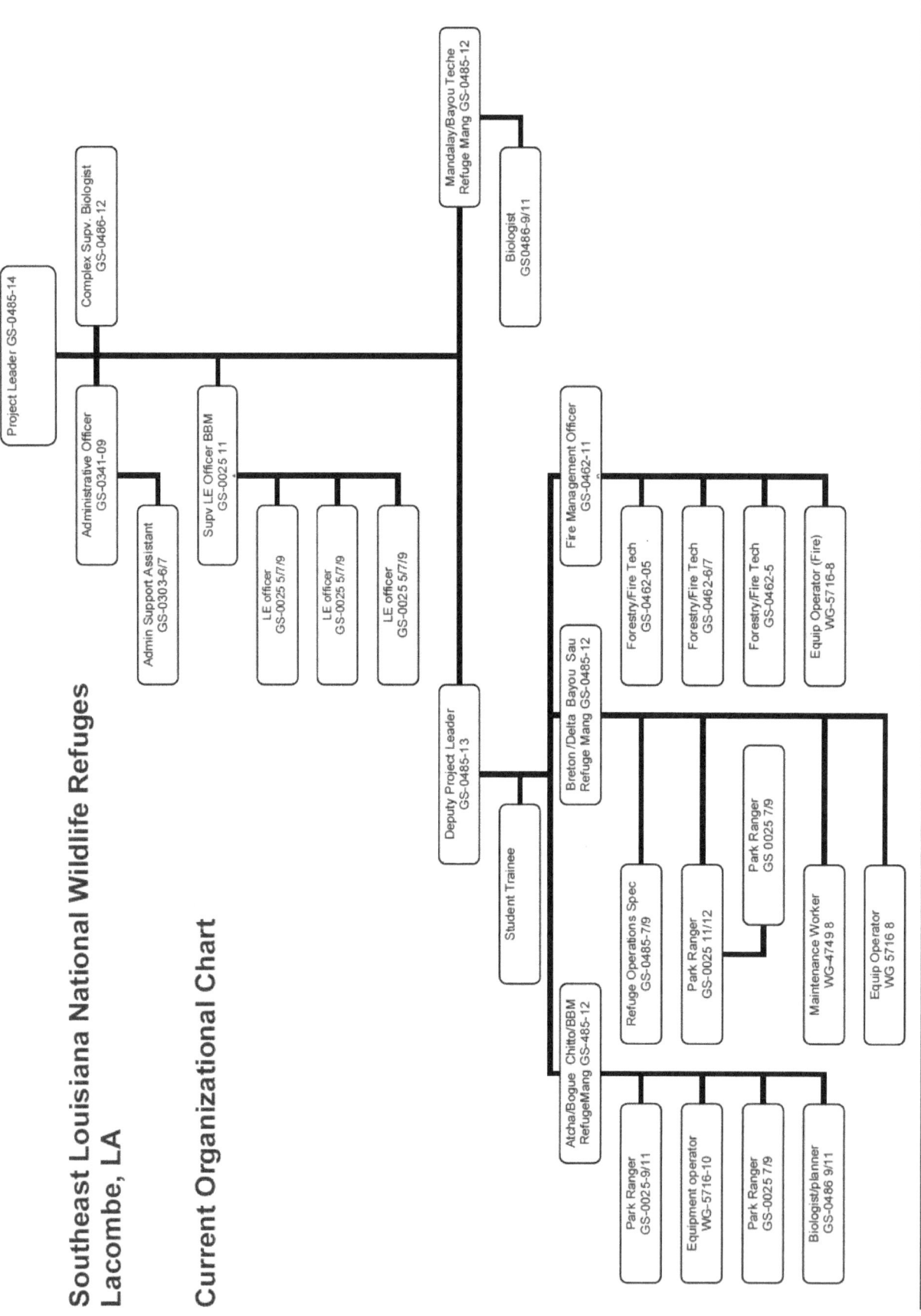

Figure 8. Proposed staffing chart for Mandalay and Bayou Teche National Wildlife Refuges

Southeast Louisiana
National Wildlife Refuges

Proposed Organizational Chart

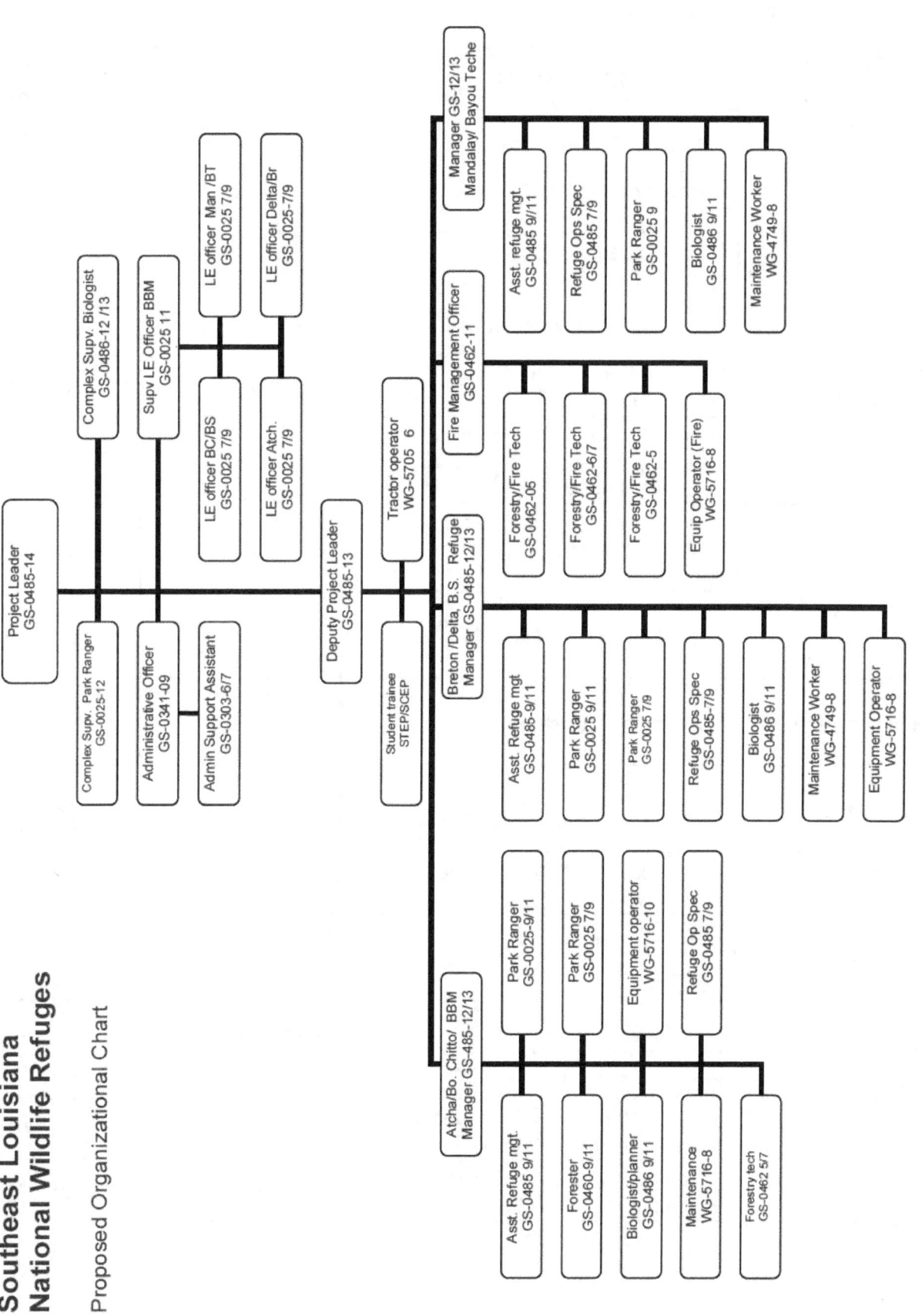

Comprehensive Conservation Plan

Table 1. Summary of proposed projects

PROJECT NUMBER	PROJECT TITLE	FIRST YEAR COST	RECURRING ANNUAL COST
Populations 1 Mandalay	Monitor waterfowl usage	$5,000	$2,000
Populations 2 Mandalay	Monitor and manage trust resource populations	$20,000	$8,000
Populations 3 Mandalay	Provide brood habitat and nest sites for wood ducks	$5,000	$1,000
Habitat 1 Mandalay	Restore marsh in open ponds	$15,000,000	$5,000
Habitat 2 Mandalay	Use beneficial dredge from GIWW to create marsh	$30,000,000	$5,000
Habitat 3 Mandalay	Develop monitoring for marsh loss, water depths, aquatic vegetation and public use impacts	$30,000	$2,000
Protection 1 Mandalay and Bayou Teche	Provide adequate Law Enforcement for refuge resources, species, and visitors	$90,000	$90,000
Protection 2 Mandalay and Bayou Teche	Maintain boundary markers	$200,000	$5,000
Protection 3 Mandalay and Bayou Teche	Maintain infrastructure	$200,000	$125,000
Protection 4 Mandalay and Bayou Teche	Administer Oil and Gas activities	$75,000	$75,000
Protection 5	Acquire lands within acquisition boundary	Unknown	Unknown
Visitor Services 1 Mandalay	Maintain facilities	$10,000	$10,000
Visitor Services 2 Mandalay	Improve visitor services and interpretation	$60,000	$5,000
Visitor Services 3 Mandalay	Improve and enhance hunting and fishing opportunities	$10,000	$10,000
Visitor Services 4 Mandalay	Provide/improve wildlife observation and photography opportunities	$15,000	$2,000
Visitor Services 5 Mandalay	Increase public outreach and environmental education	$75,000	$75,000

PARTNERSHIP/VOLUNTEERS OPPORTUNITIES

A key element of this CCP is to establish partnerships with local volunteers, landowners, private organizations, and state and federal natural resource agencies. Partnerships are critically important to achieve refuge goals, leverage funds, minimize costs, reduce redundancy, and bridge relationships. In the immediate vicinity of Mandalay NWR, opportunities exist to establish and maintain partnerships with LDWF in law enforcement, local businesses, Terrebonne Parish Consolidated Government, city of Houma, Houma Area Convention and Visitor's Bureau, the Nature Conservancy, Terrebonne Bird Club, Barataria-Terrebonne National Estuary Program, Bayou Bow-hunters Association, Ducks Unlimited, Louisiana Department of Natural Resources, and local universities.

The refuge staff can work with neighboring private landowners through the Partners Program or through agreements for managing neighboring land to complement the refuge management program.

STEP-DOWN MANAGEMENT PLANS

A CCP is a strategic plan that guides the direction of the refuge. A step-down management plan provides specific guidance on activities, such as habitat management and visitor services. These plans (Tables 2 and 3) are also developed in accordance with the National Environmental Policy Act, which requires the identification and evaluation of alternatives and public review and involvement prior to their implementation.

Table 2. Mandalay National Wildlife Refuge step-down management plans related to the goals and objectives of the comprehensive conservation plan

Step-down Plan	Completion Date	Revision Date
Fisheries management	2013	2028
Visitor Services	2015	2030
Station safety	2013	2028
Hunting plan	1999	2014
Sport Fishing plan	1999	2014
Sign plan	2015	2030
Law enforcement	2014	2029
Wildlife Inventory	2009	2024
Habitat Management	2012	2027
Hurricane/Incident Plan	2008	Annual
Nuisance species control plan	2012	2027

MONITORING AND ADAPTIVE MANAGEMENT

Adaptive management is a flexible approach to long-term management of biotic resources that is directed over time by the results of ongoing monitoring activities and other information. More specifically, adaptive management is a process by which projects are implemented within a framework of scientifically driven experiments to test the predictions and assumptions outlined within a plan.

To apply adaptive management, specific surveying, inventorying, and monitoring protocols will be adopted for the refuges. The habitat management strategies will be systematically evaluated to determine management effects on wildlife populations. This information will be used to refine approaches and determine how effectively the objectives are being accomplished. Evaluations will include ecosystem team and other appropriate partner participation. If monitoring and evaluation indicate undesirable effects for target and non-target species and/or communities, then alterations to the management projects will be made. Subsequently, this CCP will be revised. Specific monitoring and evaluation activities will be described in the step-down management plans.

PLAN REVIEW AND REVISION

This CCP will be reviewed annually as the refuge's annual work plans and budgets are developed. It will also be reviewed to determine the need for revision. A revision will occur if and when conditions change or significant information becomes available, such as a change in ecological conditions or a major refuge expansion. The final CCP will be augmented by detailed step-down management plans to address the completion of specific strategies in support of the refuge's goals and objectives. Revisions to this CCP and the step-down management plans will be subject to public review and NEPA compliance.

Appendix A. Glossary

Adaptive Management:	Refers to a process in which policy decisions are implemented within a framework of scientifically driven experiments to test predictions and assumptions inherent in a management plan. Analysis of results helps managers determine whether current management should continue as is or whether it should be modified to achieve desired conditions.
Alluvial:	Sediment transported and deposited in a delta or riverbed by flowing water.
Alternative:	1. A reasonable way to fix the identified problem or satisfy the stated need (40 CFR 1500.2). 2. Alternatives are different sets of objectives and strategies or means of achieving refuge purposes and goals, helping fulfill the Refuge System mission, and resolving issues (Service Manual 602 FW 1.6B).
Anadromous:	Migratory fishes that spend most of their lives in the sea and migrate to fresh water to breed.
Approved Acquisition Boundary:	A project boundary which the Director of the Fish and Wildlife Service approves upon completion of a detailed planning and environmental compliance process.
Biological Diversity:	The variety of life and its processes, including the variety of living organisms, the genetic differences among them, and the communities and ecosystems in which they occur (Service Manual 052 FW 1. 12B). The System's focus is on indigenous species, biotic communities, and ecological processes. Also referred to as biodiversity.
Biological Integrity:	The biotic composition, structure, and functioning at genetic, organism, and community levels comparable with historic conditions including the natural biological processes that shape genomes, organisms, and communities.
Brackish Marsh:	Marshes occurring where salinity ranges from 3-15 parts per thousand (ppt); dominated by wiregrass.
Categorical Exclusion:	A category of actions that does not individually or cumulatively have a significant effect on the human environment and have been found to have no such effect in procedures adopted by a federal agency pursuant to the National Environmental Policy Act (40 CFR 1508.4).
CFR:	Code of Federal Regulations.

Compatible Use: A proposed or existing wildlife-dependent recreational use or any other use of a national wildlife refuge that, based on sound professional judgment, will not materially interfere with or detract from the fulfillment of the National Wildlife Refuge System mission or the purpose(s) of the national wildlife refuge [50 CFR 25.12 (a)]. A compatibility determination supports the selection of compatible uses and identifies stipulations or limits necessary to ensure compatibility.

Comprehensive Conservation Plan: A document that describes the desired future conditions of a refuge or planning unit and provides long-range guidance and management direction to achieve the purposes of the refuge; helps fulfill the mission of the Refuge System; maintains and, where appropriate, restores the ecological integrity of each refuge and the Refuge System; helps achieve the goals of the National Wilderness Preservation System; and meets other mandates (Service Manual 602 FW 1.6 E).

Concern: See Issue

Cover Type: The present vegetation of an area.

Cultural Resource Inventory: A professionally conducted study designed to locate and evaluate evidence of cultural resources present within a defined geographic area. Inventories may involve various levels, including background literature search, comprehensive field examination to identify all exposed physical manifestations of cultural resources, or sample inventory to project site distribution and density over a larger area. Evaluation of identified cultural resources to determine eligibility for the National Register follows the criteria found in 36 CFR 60.4 (Service Manual 614 FW 1.7).

Cultural Resource Overview: A comprehensive document prepared for a field office that discusses, among other things, its prehistory and cultural history, the nature and extent of known cultural resources, previous research, management objectives, resource management conflicts or issues, and a general statement on how program objectives should be met and conflicts resolved. An overview should reference or incorporate information from a field office's background or literature search described in Section VIII of the Cultural Resource Management Handbook (Service Manual 614 FW 1.7).

Cultural Resources: The remains of sites, structures, or objects used by people in the past.

Designated Wilderness Area: An area designated by the U.S. Congress to be managed as part of the National Wilderness Preservation System (Draft Service Manual 610 FW 1.5).

Disturbance: Significant alteration of habitat structure or composition. May be natural (e.g., fire) or human-caused events (e.g., aircraft overflight).

Diurnal Range:	The difference in height between mean higher high water and mean lower low water.
Dredging:	The removal of sediment (spoil) from a channel to produce sufficient depths for navigation.
Ecosystem:	A dynamic and interrelating complex of plant and animal communities and their associated non-living environment.
Ecosystem Management:	Management of natural resources using system-wide concepts to ensure that all plants and animals in ecosystems are maintained at viable levels in native habitats and basic ecosystem processes are perpetuated indefinitely.
Endangered Species (Federal):	A plant or animal species listed under the Endangered Species Act that is in danger of extinction throughout all or a significant portion of its range.
Endangered Species (State):	A plant or animal species in danger of becoming extinct or extirpated in the state within the near future if factors contributing to its decline continue. Populations of these species are at critically low levels or their habitats have been degraded or depleted to a significant degree.
Endemic	An organism being exclusively native to a place or biota.
Environmental Assessment (EA):	A concise public document, prepared in compliance with the National Environmental Policy Act, that briefly discusses the purpose and need for an action, alternatives to such action, and provides sufficient evidence and analysis of impacts to determine whether to prepare an environmental impact statement or finding of no significant impact (40 CFR 1508.9).
Environmental Impact Statement (EIS):	A detailed written statement required by section 102(2)(C) of the National Environmental Policy Act, analyzing the environmental impacts of a proposed action, adverse effects of the project that cannot be avoided, alternative courses of action, short-term uses of the environment versus the maintenance and enhancement of long-term productivity, and any irreversible and irretrievable commitment of resources (40 CFR 1508.11).
Estuary:	The wide lower course of a river into which the tides flow. The area where the tide meets a river current.
Fast Lands:	Land which is above the mean or ordinary high tide line; also called uplands.

Finding of No Significant Impact (FONSI): A document prepared in compliance with the National Environmental Policy Act, supported by an environmental assessment, that briefly presents why a federal action will have no significant effect on the human environment and for which an environmental impact statement, therefore, will not be prepared (40 CFR 1508.13).

Forest Fragmentation: A form of habitat fragmentation, occurring when forests are cut down in a manner that leaves relatively small, isolated patches of forest know as fragments or remnants.

Goal: Descriptive, open-ended, and often broad statement of desired future conditions that conveys a purpose but does not define measurable units (Service Manual 620 FW 1.6J).

Habitat: Suite of existing environmental conditions required by an organism for survival and reproduction. The place where an organism typically lives.

Habitat Restoration: Management emphasis designed to move ecosystems to desired conditions and processes, and/or to healthy ecosystems.

Habitat Type: See Vegetation Type.

Hypoxic Zone: An area located along the Louisiana-Texas coast in which water near the bottom of the Gulf contains less than 2 parts per million of dissolved oxygen, causing stress or even death to bottom dwelling organisms.

Improvement Act: The National Wildlife Refuge System Improvement Act of 1997.

Informed Consent: The grudging willingness of opponents to "go along" with a course of action that they actually oppose (Bleiker).

Issue: Any unsettled matter that requires a management decision [e.g., an initiative, opportunity, resource management problem, threat to the resources of the unit, conflict in uses, public concern, or other presence of an undesirable resource condition (Service Manual 602 FW 1.6K)].

Management Alternative: See Alternative

Management Concern: See Issue

Management Opportunity: See Issue

Migration: The seasonal movement from one area to another and back.

Mission Statement:	Succinct statement of the unit's purpose and reason for being.
Monitoring:	The process of collecting information to track changes of selected parameters over time.
National Environmental Policy Act of 1969 (NEPA):	Requires all agencies, including the Service, to examine the environmental impacts of their actions, incorporate environmental information, and use public participation in the planning and implementation of all actions. Federal agencies must integrate NEPA with other planning requirements, and prepare appropriate NEPA documents to facilitate better environmental decision-making (40 CFR 1500).
National Wildlife Refuge System Improvement Act of 1997 (Public Law 105-57):	Under the Refuge Improvement Act, the Fish and Wildlife Service is required to develop 15-year comprehensive conservation plans for all national wildlife refuges outside Alaska. The Act also describes the six public uses given priority status within the Refuge System (i.e., hunting, fishing, wildlife observation, wildlife photography, and environmental education and interpretation).
National Wildlife Refuge System Mission:	The mission is to administer a national network of lands and waters for the conservation, management, and where appropriate, restoration of the fish, wildlife, and plant resources and their habitats within the United States for the benefit of present and future generations of Americans.
National Wildlife Refuge System:	Various categories of areas administered by the Secretary of the Interior for the conservation of fish and wildlife, including species threatened with extinction; all lands, waters, and interests therein administered by the Secretary as wildlife refuges; areas for the protection and conservation of fish and wildlife that are threatened with extinction; wildlife ranges; game ranges; wildlife management areas; or waterfowl production areas.
National Wildlife Refuge:	A designated area of land, water, or an interest in land or water within the Refuge System.
Native Species:	Species that normally live and thrive in a particular ecosystem.
Noxious Weed:	A plant species designated by federal or state law as generally possessing one or more of the following characteristics: aggressive or difficult to manage; parasitic; a carrier or host of serious insect or disease; or non-native, new, or not common to the United States. According to the Federal Noxious Weed Act (P.L. 93-639), a noxious weed is one that causes disease or had adverse effects on man or his environment and therefore is detrimental to the agriculture and commerce of the Untied States and to the public health.

Objective:	A concise statement of what we want to achieve, how much we want to achieve, when and where we want to achieve it, and who is responsible for the work. Objectives derive from goals and provide the basis for determining strategies, monitoring refuge accomplishments, and evaluating the success of strategies. Making objectives attainable, time-specific, and measurable (Service Manual 602 FW 1.6N).
Plant Association:	A classification of plant communities based on the similarity in dominants of all layers of vascular species in a climax community.
Plant Community:	An assemblage of plant species unique in its composition; occurs in particular locations under particular influences; a reflection or integration of the environmental influences on the site such as soils, temperature, elevation, solar radiation, slope, aspect, and rainfall; denotes a general kind of climax plant community.
Preferred Alternative:	This is the alternative determined (by the decision-maker) to best achieve the refuge purpose, vision, and goals; contributes to the Refuge System mission, addresses the significant issues; and is consistent with principles of sound fish and wildlife management.
Prescribed Fire:	The application of fire to wildland fuels to achieve identified land use objectives (Service Manual 621 FW 1.7). May occur from natural ignition or intentional ignition.
Priority Species:	Fish and wildlife species that require protective measures and/or management guidelines to ensure their perpetuation. Priority species include the following: (1) State-listed and candidate species; (2) species or groups of animals susceptible to significant population declines within a specific area or statewide by virtue of their inclination to aggregate (e.g., seabird colonies); and (3) species of recreation, commercial, and/or tribal importance.
Public Involvement Plan:	Broad long-term guidance for involving the public in the comprehensive conservation planning process.
Public Involvement:	A process that offers impacted and interested individuals and organizations an opportunity to become informed about, and to express their opinions on Service actions and policies. In the process, these views are studied thoroughly and thoughtful consideration of public views is given in shaping decisions for refuge management.
Public:	Individuals, organizations, and groups; officials of federal, state, and local government agencies; Indian tribes; and foreign nations. It may include anyone outside the core planning team. It includes those who may or may not have indicated an interest in service issues and those who do or do not realize that Service decisions may affect them.

Purposes of the Refuge:	"The purposes specified in or derived from the law, proclamation, executive order, agreement, public land order, donation document, or administrative memorandum establishing, authorizing, or expanding a refuge, refuge unit, or refuge sub-unit." For refuges that encompass congressionally designated wilderness, the purposes of the Wilderness Act are additional purposes of the refuge (Service Manual 602 FW 106 S).
Recommended Wilderness:	Areas studied and found suitable for wilderness designation by both the Director of the Fish and Wildlife Service and the Secretary of the Department of the Interior, and recommended for designation by the President to Congress. These areas await only legislative action by Congress in order to become part of the Wilderness System. Such areas are also referred to as "pending in Congress" (Draft Service Manual 610 FW 1.5).
Record of Decision (ROD):	A concise public record of decision prepared by the federal agency, pursuant to NEPA, that contains a statement of the decision, identification of all alternatives considered, identification of the environmentally preferable alternative, a statement as to whether all practical means to avoid or minimize environmental harm from the alternative selected have been adopted (and if not, why they were not), and a summary of monitoring and enforcement where applicable for any mitigation 40 CFR 1505.2).
Refuge Goal:	See Goal
Refuge Purposes:	See Purposes of the Refuge
Saltwater Intrusion:	The invasion of freshwater bodies by denser salt water.
Sea-level Rise:	A rise in the surface of the sea due to increased water volume of the ocean and/or sinking of the land.
Shoreline Progradation:	A shoreline that is being built seaward by accumulation of deposition.
Songbirds: (Also Passerines)	A category of birds that is medium to small, perching landbirds. Most are territorial singers and migratory.
Step-down Management Plan:	A plan that provides specific guidance on management subjects (e.g., habitat, public use, fire, and safety) or groups of related subjects. It describes strategies and implementation schedules for meeting CCP goals and objectives (Service Manual 602 FW 1.6 U).
Strategy:	A specific action, tool, technique, or combination of actions, tools, and techniques used to meet unit objectives (Service Manual 602 FW 1.6 U).

Study Area:
The area reviewed in detail for wildlife, habitat, and public use potential. For purposes of this CCP, the study area includes the lands within the currently approved refuge boundary and potential refuge expansion areas.

Subsidence:
A gradual sinking of land with respect to its previous level.

Threatened Species (Federal):
Species listed under the Endangered Species Act that are likely to become endangered within the foreseeable future throughout all or a significant portion of their range.

Threatened Species (State):
A plant or animal species likely to become endangered in the state within the near future if factors contributing to population decline or habitat degradation or loss continue.

Tiering:
The coverage of general matters in broader environmental impact statements with subsequent narrower statements of environmental analysis, incorporating by reference, the general discussions and concentrating on specific issues (40 CFR 1508.28).

U.S. Fish and Wildlife Service Mission:
The mission of the U.S. Fish and Wildlife Service is working with others to conserve, protect, and enhance fish and wildlife and their habitats for the continuing benefit of the American people.

Unit Objective:
See Objective

Vegetation Type, Habitat Type, Forest Cover Type:
A land classification system based upon the concept of distinct plant associations.

Vision Statement:
A concise statement of what the planning unit should be, or what we hope to do, based primarily upon the Refuge System mission and specific refuge purposes, and other mandates. We will tie the vision statement for the refuge to the mission of the Refuge System; the purpose(s) of the refuge; the maintenance or restoration of the ecological integrity of each refuge and the Refuge System; and other mandates (Service Manual 602 FW 1.6 Z).

Wilderness Study Areas:

Lands and waters identified through inventory as meeting the definition of wilderness and undergoing evaluation for recommendation for inclusion in the Wilderness System. A study area must meet the following criteria:

- Generally appears to have been affected primarily by the forces of nature, with the imprint of man's work substantially unnoticeable;

- Has outstanding opportunities for solitude or a primitive and unconfined type of recreation; and

- Has at least 5,000 contiguous roadless acres or is sufficient in size as to make practicable its preservation and use in an unimpaired condition (Draft Service Manual 610 FW 1.5).

Wilderness:

See Designated Wilderness

Wildfire:

A free-burning fire requiring a suppression response; all fire other than prescribed fire that occurs on wildlands (Service Manual 621 FW 1.7).

ACRONYMS AND ABBREVIATIONS

BBCC Black Bear Conservation Committee
BCC Birds of Conservation Concern
BRT Biological Review Team
BTNEP Barataria - Terrebone National Estuary Program
CCP Comprehensive Conservation Plan
CFR Code of Federal Regulations
CIAP Coastal Impact Assistance Program
CMZ Coastal Management Zone
CWPPRA Coastal Wetlands Planning, Protection and Restoration Act
cfs cubic feet per second
DNR Louisiana Department of Natural Resources
DOI Department of the Interior
DOTD Department of Transportation and Development
DU Ducks Unlimited
EA Environmental Assessment
EE environmental education
EIS Environmental Impact Statement
EPA U.S. Environmental Protection Agency
ESA Endangered Species Act
FR Federal Register
FTE full-time equivalent (STAFF)
FY Fiscal Year
GIS Global Information System
GIWW Gulf Intracoastal Waterway
GOCA Governor's Office on Coastal Activities
LCA Louisiana Coastal Area Ecosystem Restoration Study
NAWCA North American Wetlands Conservation Act
NAWMP North American Waterfowl Management Plan
NEPA National Environmental Policy Act
NRCS Natural Resource Conservation Service
NRHP National Register of Historic Places
NWR National Wildlife Refuge
NWRS National Wildlife Refuge System
OPA Otherwise Protected Area
PFT Permanent Full Time
RM Refuge Manual
RNA Research Natural Area
ROD Record of Decision
RONS Refuge Operating Needs System
RRP Refuge Roads Program
Service U.S. Fish and Wildlife Service (also, FWS)
SLAMM Sea-level Affecting Marshes Model
TFT Temporary Full Time
USC United States Code
USFS U. S. Forest Service
USFWS U.S. Fish and Wildlife Service

Appendix B. References and Literature Citations

Barataria Terrebonne National Estuary Program. http://btnep.org/home.asp

Bahr. L.M., Jr. 1983. Ecological Characterization of the Mississippi Deltaic Plain Region: A Narrative with Management Recommendations. U.S. Fish and Wildlife Service. 189 pp.

Black Bear Conservation Committee. 2005. "Black Bear Management Handbook for LA, MS, southern AR, and east TX". BBCC. 88pp.

Clough, J.S. 2008. Application of the Sea-Level Affecting Marshes Model (SLAMM 5.0) to Mandalay National Wildlife Refuge. Warren Pinnacle Consulting, Inc.

Clough, J.S. 2008. Application of the Sea-Level Affecting Marshes Model (SLAMM 5.0) to Bayou Teche National Wildlife Refuge. Warren Pinnacle Consulting, Inc.

Coastal Protection and Restoration Authority of Louisiana. "Integrated Ecosystem Restoration and Hurricane Protection: Louisiana's Comprehensive Master Plan for a Sustainable Coast." 2007. http://www.lacpra.org

Coastal Wetland Forest Conservation and Use Science Working Group. "Conservation, Protection, and Mitigation of Louisiana's Coastal Wetland Forests." Final Report to the Governor of Louisiana. April 30, 2005. http://www.coastalforestswg.lsu.edu/THEFinalReport.pdf

"Coastal Wetlands Planning, Protection, and Restoration Act (CWPPRA): A Response to Louisiana's Land Loss." 2006. http://www.lacoast.gov

"Coastal Wetland Planning, Protection, and Restoration Act (CWPPRA) Restoration Projects." http://www.lacoast.gov/projects/list.asp

"Coastal Wetlands Planning, Protection, and Restoration Act (CWPPRA) Restoration Projects: PO-16 and PO-18." http://www.lacoast.gov/projects/overview.asp?statenumber=PO%2D16; and http://www.lacoast.gov/projects/overview.asp?statenumber=PO%2D18

Conservation Commission of Missouri. "Managing Wetlands: Moist-Soil Management (Seasonally Flooded Impoundments)." 2007. http://mdc.mo.gov/landown/wetland/wetmng/8.htm (accessed August 13, 2007)

Dupree, A. Hunter. 1957. Science in the Federal Government: A History of Policies and Activities to 1940. Harvard University Press, Cambridge, Massachusetts. 460 pp.

Eyre, F.H. 1980. Forest Cover Types of the United States and Canada. Society of American Foresters, Washington, DC. 148 pp.

Gabrielson, Ira N. 1943. Wildlife Conservation. The Macmillan Company, New York, New York. 250 pp.

Laycock, George. 1965. The Sign of the Flying Goose: A Guide to the National Wildlife Refuges. The Natural History Press, Garden City, New York. 299 pp.

Louisiana Coastal Wetlands Conservation and Restoration Task Force. 2001. The 2000 Evaluation Report to the US Congress on the effectiveness of Louisiana Coastal Wetland Restoration Projects. Baton Rouge, LA: Louisiana Department of Natural Resources. 85 pp.

Louisiana Department of Natural Resources. 1996. Louisiana Coast Lines Publication. http://www.dnr.state.la.us/crm/coastmgt/coastlines/1996-12.htm.

Louisiana Department of Wildlife and Fisheries. 1988. Louisiana Coastal Marsh Vegetative Type Maps. Prepared by Robert H. Chabreck and Greg Linscombe

Louisiana Department of Wildlife and Fisheries. 2007. Nutria. http://www.nutria.com/site.php.

Louisiana Department of Wildlife and FIsheries. 2004. Strategic Plan 2006-2010. 38 pp.

Louisiana Department of Wildlife and Fisheries. 2005. Louisiana Comprehensive Wildlife Consrvation Strategy (Wildlife Action Plan). 455 pp.

Louisiana Wildlife and Fisheries Commission. 1971. Cooperative Gulf of Mexico Estuarine Inventory and Study, Louisiana. 175 pp.

Meretsky, V.J., et al. 2006. New Directions in Conservation for the National Wildlife Refuge System. Bio Science Vol. 56 No. 2. pp135-143

New Employee Handbook. U.S. Fish and Wildlife Service.

U.S. Army Corps of Engineers. 1998. Water Resources Development in Louisiana. 177p

U.S. Army Corps of Enginerrs. 1977. Land's End, A History of the New Orleans District, U.S. Army Corps of Engineers, and Its Lifelong Battle with the Lower Mississippi and Other Rivers Winding Their Way to the Sea. 118 pp.

U.S. Census Bureau. 2000. State and County Quick Facts. U.S. Census Bureau website http://quickfacts.census.gov/qfd/states/22/22103.html.

U.S. Fish and Wildlife Service. 2008. Critical habitat for the Louisiana black bear. Federal Register, May 6, 2008 (73 FR 25354)

U.S. Fish and Wildlife Service. 2006. Mandalay National Wildlife Refuge, Biological Review, October 31, 2006.

U.S. Fish and Wildlife Service. 2006. Bayou Teche National Wildlife Refuge, Biological Review, November 1 and 2, 2006.
U.S. Fish and Wildlife Service. 2006. Public Use Review Report, Mandalay and Bayou Teche National Wildlife Refuges, 2006.

Appendix C. Relevant Legal Mandates and Executive Orders

STATUE	DESCRIPTION
Administrative Procedures Act (1946)	Outlines administrative procedures to be followed by federal agencies with respect to identification of information to be made public; publication of material in the Federal Register; maintenance of records; attendance and notification requirements for specific meetings and hearings; issuance of licenses; and review of agency actions.
American Antiquities Act of 1906	Provides penalties for unauthorized collection, excavation, or destruction of historic or prehistoric ruins, monuments, or objects of antiquity on lands owned or controlled by the United States. The Act authorizes the President to designate as national monuments objects or areas of historic or scientific interest on lands owned or controlled by the Unites States.
American Indian Religious Freedom Act of 1978	Protects the inherent right of Native Americans to believe, express, and exercise their traditional religions, including access to important sites, use and possession of sacred objects, and the freedom to worship through ceremonial and traditional rites.
Americans With Disabilities Act of 1990	Intended to prevent discrimination of and make American society more accessible to people with disabilities. The Act requires reasonable accommodations to be made in employment, public services, public accommodations, and telecommunications for persons with disabilities.
Anadromous Fish Conservation Act of 1965, as amended	Authorizes the Secretaries of Interior and Commerce to enter into cooperative agreements with states and other non-federal interests for conservation, development, and enhancement of anadromous fish and contribute up to 50 percent as the federal share of the cost of carrying out such agreements. Reclamation construction programs for water resource projects needed solely for such fish are also authorized.
Archaeological Resources Protection Act of 1979, as amended.	This Act strengthens and expands the protective provisions of the Antiquities Act of 1906 regarding archaeological resources. It also revised the permitting process for archaeological research.
Architectural Barriers Act of 1968	Requires that buildings and facilities designed, constructed, or altered with federal funds, or leased by a federal agency, must comply with standards for physical accessibility.

STATUE	DESCRIPTION
Bald and Golden Eagle Protection Act of 1940, as amended	Prohibits the possession, sale or transport of any bald or golden eagle, alive or dead, or part, nest, or egg except as permitted by the Secretary of the Interior for scientific or exhibition purposes, or for the religious purposes of Indians.
Bankhead-Jones Farm Tenant Act of 1937	Directs the Secretary of Agriculture to develop a program of land conservation and utilization in order to correct maladjustments in land use and thus assist in such things as control of soil erosion, reforestation, conservation of natural resources and protection of fish and wildlife. Some early refuges and hatcheries were established under authority of this Act.
Cave Resources Protection Act of 1988	Established requirements for the management and protection of caves and their resources on federal lands, including allowing the land managing agencies to withhold the location of caves from the public, and requiring permits for any removal or collecting activities in caves on federal lands.
Clean Air Act of 1970	Regulates air emissions from area, stationary, and mobile sources. This Act and its amendments charge federal land managers with direct responsibility to protect the "air quality and related values" of land under their control. These values include fish, wildlife, and their habitats.
Clean Water Act of 1974, as amended	This Act and its amendments have as its objective the restoration and maintenance of the chemical, physical, and biological integrity of the Nation's waters. Section 401 of the Act requires that federally permitted activities comply with the Clean Water Act standards, state water quality laws, and any other appropriate state laws. Section 404 charges the U.S. Army Corps of Engineers with regulating discharge of dredge or fill materials into waters of the United States, including wetlands.
Coastal Barrier Resources Act of 1982 (CBRA)	Identifies undeveloped coastal barriers along the Atlantic and Gulf Coasts and included them in the John H. Chafee Coastal Barrier Resources System (CBRS). The objectives of the act are to minimize loss of human life, reduce wasteful federal expenditures, and minimize the damage to natural resources by restricting most federal expenditures that encourage development within the CBRS.
Coastal Barrier Improvement Act of 1990	Reauthorized the Coastal Barrier Resources Act (CBRA), expanded the CBRS to include undeveloped coastal barriers along the Great Lakes and in the Caribbean, and established "Otherwise Protected Areas (OPAs)." The Service is responsible for maintaining official maps, consulting with federal agencies that propose spending federal funds within the CBRS and OPAs, and making recommendations to Congress about proposed boundary revisions.

STATUE	DESCRIPTION
Coastal Wetlands Planning, Protection, and Restoration (1990)	Authorizes the Director of the Fish and Wildlife Service to participate in the development of a Louisiana coastal wetlands restoration program, participate in the development and oversight of a coastal wetlands conservation program, and lead in the implementation and administration of a national coastal wetlands grant program.
Coastal Zone Management Act of 1972, as amended	Established a voluntary national program within the Department of Commerce to encourage coastal states to develop and implement coastal zone management plans and requires that "any federal activity within or outside of the coastal zone that affects any land or water use or natural resource of the coastal zone" shall be "consistent to the maximum extent practicable with the enforceable policies" of a state's coastal zone management plan. The law includes an Enhancement Grants Program for protecting, restoring, or enhancing existing coastal wetlands or creating new coastal wetlands. It also established the National Estuarine Research Reserve System, guidelines for estuarine research, and financial assistance for land acquisition.
Emergency Wetlands Resources Act of 1986	This Act authorized the purchase of wetlands from Land and Water Conservation Fund moneys, removing a prior prohibition on such acquisitions. The Act requires the Secretary to establish a National Wetlands Priority Conservation Plan, required the states to include wetlands in their Comprehensive Outdoor Recreation Plans, and transfers to the Migratory Bird Conservation Fund amounts equal to import duties on arms and ammunition. It also established entrance fees at national wildlife refuges.
Endangered Species Act of 1973, as amended	Provides for the conservation of threatened and endangered species of fish, wildlife, and plants by federal action and by encouraging the establishment of state programs. It provides for the determination and listing of threatened and endangered species and the designation of critical habitats. Section 7 requires refuge managers to perform internal consultation before initiating projects that affect or may affect endangered species.
Environmental Education Act of 1990	This Act established the Office of Environmental Education within the U.S. Environmental Protection Agency to develop and administer a federal environmental education program in consultation with other federal natural resource management agencies, including the Fish and Wildlife Service.

STATUE	DESCRIPTION
Estuary Protection Act of 1968	Authorized the Secretary of the Interior, in cooperation with other federal agencies and the states, to study and inventory estuaries of the United States, including land and water of the Great Lakes, and to determine whether such areas should be acquired for protection. The Secretary is also required to encourage state and local governments to consider the importance of estuaries in their planning activities relative to federal natural resource grants. In approving any state grants for acquisition of estuaries, the Secretary was required to establish conditions to ensure the permanent protection of estuaries.
Estuaries and Clean Waters Act of 2000	This law creates a federal interagency council that includes the Director of the Fish and Wildlife Service, the Secretary of the Army for Civil Works, the Secretary of Agriculture, the Administrator of the Environmental Protection Agency and the Administrator for the National Oceanic and Atmospheric Administration. The council is charged with developing a national estuary habitat restoration strategy and providing grants to entities to restore and protect estuary habitat to promote the strategy.
Food Security Act of 1985, as amended (Farm Bill)	The Act contains several provisions that contribute to wetland conservation. The Swampbuster provisions state that farmers who convert wetlands for the purpose of planting after enactment of the law are ineligible for most farmer program subsidies. It also established the Wetland Reserve Program to restore and protect wetlands through easements and restoration of the functions and values of wetlands on such easement areas.
Farmland Protection Policy Act of 1981, as amended	The purpose of this law is to minimize the extent to which federal programs contribute to the unnecessary conversion of farmland to nonagricultural uses. Federal programs include construction projects and the management of federal lands.
Federal Advisory Committee Act (1972), as amended	Governs the establishment of and procedures for committees that provide advice to the federal government. Advisory committees may be established only if they will serve a necessary, nonduplicative function. Committees must be strictly advisory unless otherwise specified and meetings must be open to the public.
Federal Coal Leasing Amendment Act of 1976	Provided that nothing in the Mining Act, the Mineral Leasing Act, or the Mineral Leasing Act for Acquired Lands authorized mining coal on refuges.
Federal-Aid Highways Act of 1968	Established requirements for approval of federal highways through national wildlife refuges and other designated areas to preserve the natural beauty of such areas. The Secretary of Transportation is directed to consult with the Secretary of the Interior and other federal agencies before approving any program or project requiring the use of land under their jurisdiction.

STATUE	DESCRIPTION
Federal Noxious Weed Act of 1990, as amended	The Secretary of Agriculture was given the authority to designate plants as noxious weeds and to cooperate with other federal, State and local agencies, farmers' associations, and private individuals in measures to control, eradicate, prevent, or retard the spread of such weeds. The Act requires each Federal land-managing agency, including the Fish and Wildlife Service, to designate an office or person to coordinate a program to control such plants on the agency's land and implement cooperative agreements with the states, including integrated management systems to control undesirable plants.
Fish and Wildlife Act of 1956	Establishes a comprehensive national fish, shellfish, and wildlife resources policy with emphasis on the commercial fishing industry but also includes the inherent right of every citizen and resident to fish for pleasure, enjoyment, and betterment and to maintain and increase public opportunities for recreational use of fish and wildlife resources. Among other things, it authorizes the Secretary of the Interior to take such steps as may be required for the development, advancement, management, conservation, and protection of fish and wildlife resources including, but not limited to, research, development of existing facilities, and acquisition by purchase or exchange of land and water or interests therein.
Fish and Wildlife Conservation Act of 1980, as amended	Requires the Service to monitor non-gamebird species, identify species of management concern, and implement conservation measures to preclude the need for listing under the Endangered Species Act.
Fish and Wildlife Coordination Act of 1958	Promotes equal consideration and coordination of wildlife conservation with other water resource development programs by requiring consultation with the Fish and Wildlife Service and the state fish and wildlife agencies where the "waters of a stream or other body of water are proposed or authorized, permitted or licensed to be impounded, diverted…or otherwise controlled or modified" by any agency under federal permit or license.
Improvement Act of 1978	This act was passed to improve the administration of fish and wildlife programs and amends several earlier laws, including the Refuge Recreation Act, the National Wildlife Refuge System Administration Act, and the Fish and Wildlife Act of 1956. It authorizes the Secretary to accept gifts and bequests of real and personal property on behalf of the United States. It also authorizes the use of volunteers on Service projects and appropriations to carry out volunteer programs.
Fishery (Magnuson) Conservation and Management Act of 1976	Established Regional Fishery Management Councils comprised of federal and state officials, including the Fish and Wildlife Service. It provides for regulation of foreign fishing and vessel fishing permits.

STATUE	DESCRIPTION
Freedom of Information Act, 1966	Requires all federal agencies to make available to the public for inspection and copying administrative staff manuals and staff instructions; official, published and unpublished policy statements; final orders deciding case adjudication; and other documents. Special exemptions have been reserved for nine categories of privileged material. The Act requires the party seeking the information to pay reasonable search and duplication costs.
Geothermal Steam Act of 1970, as amended	Authorizes and governs the lease of geothermal steam and related resources on public lands. Section 15 c of the Act prohibits issuing geothermal leases on virtually all Service-administrative lands.
Lacey Act of 1900, as amended	Originally designed to help states protect their native game animals and to safeguard U.S. crop production from harmful foreign species, this Act prohibits interstate and international transport and commerce of fish, wildlife or plants taken in violation of domestic or foreign laws. It regulates the introduction to America of foreign species.
Land and Water Conservation Fund Act of 1948	This Act provides funding through receipts from the sale of surplus federal land, appropriations from oil and gas receipts from the outer continental shelf, and other sources for land acquisition under several authorities. Appropriations from the fund may be used for matching grants to states for outdoor recreation projects and for land acquisition by various federal agencies, including the Fish and Wildlife Service.
Marine Mammal Protection Act of 1972, as amended	The 1972 Marine Mammal Protection Act established a federal responsibility to conserve marine mammals with management vested in the Department of the Interior for sea otter, walrus, polar bear, dugong, and manatee. The Department of Commerce is responsible for cetaceans and pinnipeds, other than the walrus. With certain specified exceptions, the Act establishes a moratorium on the taking and importation of marine mammals, as well as products taken from them.
Migratory Bird Conservation Act of 1929	Established a Migratory Bird Conservation Commission to approve areas recommended by the Secretary of the Interior for acquisition with Migratory Bird Conservation Funds. The role of the commission was expanded by the North American Wetland Conservation Act to include approving wetlands acquisition, restoration, and enhancement proposals recommended by the North American Wetlands Conservation Council.
Migratory Bird Hunting and Conservation Stamp Act of 1934	Also commonly referred to as the "Duck Stamp Act," requires waterfowl hunters 16 years of age or older to possess a valid federal hunting stamp. Receipts from the sale of the stamp are deposited into the Migratory Bird Conservation Fund for the acquisition of migratory bird refuges.

STATUE	DESCRIPTION
Migratory Bird Treaty Act of 1918, as amended	This Act implements various treaties and conventions between the United States and Canada, Japan, Mexico, and the former Soviet Union for the protection of migratory birds. Except as allowed by special regulations, this Act makes it unlawful to pursue, hunt, kill, capture, possess, buy, sell, purchase, barter, export or import any migratory bird, part, nest, egg, or product.
Mineral Leasing Act for Acquired Lands (1947), as amended	Authorizes and governs mineral leasing on acquired public lands.
Minerals Leasing Act of 1920, as amended	Authorizes and governs leasing of public lands for development of deposits of coal, oil, gas, and other hydrocarbons; sulphur; phosphate; potassium; and sodium. Section 185 of this title contains provisions relating to granting rights-of-way over federal lands for pipelines.
Mining Act of 1872, as amended	Authorizes and governs prospecting and mining for the so-called "hardrock" minerals (i.e., gold and silver) on public lands.
National and Community Service Act of 1990	Authorizes several programs to engage citizens of the U.S. in full- and/or part-time projects designed to combat illiteracy and poverty, provide job skills, enhance educational skills, and fulfill environmental needs. Among other things, this law establishes the American Conservation and Youth Service Corps to engage young adults in approved human and natural resource projects, which will benefit the public or are carried out on federal or Indian lands.
National Environmental Policy Act of 1969	Requires analysis, public comment, and reporting for environmental impacts of federal actions. It stipulates the factors to be considered in environmental impact statements, and requires that federal agencies employ an interdisciplinary approach in related decision-making and develop means to ensure that unqualified environmental values are given appropriate consideration, along with economic and technical considerations.
National Historic Preservation Act of 1966, as amended	It establishes a National Register of Historic Places and a program of matching grants for preservation of significant historical features. Federal agencies are directed to take into account the effects of their actions on items or sites listed or eligible for listing in the National Register.

STATUE	DESCRIPTION
National Trails System Act (1968), as amended	Established the National Trails System to protect the recreational, scenic, and historic values of some important trails. National recreation trails may be established by the Secretaries of Interior or Agriculture on land wholly or partly within their jurisdiction, with the consent of the involved state(s), and other land managing agencies, if any. National scenic and national historic trails may only be designated by Congress. Several national trails cross units of the National Wildlife Refuge System.
National Wildlife Refuge System Administration Act of 1966	Prior to 1966, there was no single federal law that governed the administration of the various national wildlife refuges that had been established. This Act defines the National Wildlife Refuge System and authorizes the Secretary of the Interior to permit any use of a refuge provided such use is compatible with the major purposes(s) for which the refuge was established.
National Wildlife Refuge System Improvement Act of 1997	This Act amends the National Wildlife Refuge System Administration Act of 1966. This Act defines the mission of the National Wildlife Refuge System, establishes the legitimacy and appropriateness of six priority wildlife-dependent public uses, establishes a formal process for determining compatible uses of Refuge System lands, identifies the Secretary of the Interior as responsible for managing and protecting the Refuge System, and requires the development of a comprehensive conservation plan for all refuges outside of Alaska.
Native American Graves Protection and Repatriation Act of 1990	Requires federal agencies and museums to inventory, determine ownership of, and repatriate certain cultural items and human remains under their control or possession. The Act also addresses the repatriation of cultural items inadvertently discovered by construction activities on lands managed by the agency.
Neotropical Migratory Bird Conservation Act of 2000	Establishes a matching grant program to fund projects that promote the conservation of neotropical migratory birds in the united States, Latin America, and the Caribbean.
North American Wetlands Conservation Act of 1989	Provides funding and administrative direction for implementation of the North American Waterfowl Management Plan and the Tripartite Agreement on wetlands between Canada, the United States, and Mexico. The North American Wetlands Conservation Council was created to recommend projects to be funded under the Act to the Migratory Bird Conservation Commission. Available funds may be expended for up to 50 percent of the United States' share cost of wetlands conservation projects in Canada, Mexico, or the United States (or 100 percent of the cost of projects on federal lands).

STATUE	DESCRIPTION
Refuge Recreation Act of 1962, as amended	This Act authorizes the Secretary of the Interior to administer refuges, hatcheries, and other conservation areas for recreational use, when such uses do not interfere with the area's primary purposes. It authorizes construction and maintenance of recreational facilities and the acquisition of land for incidental fish and wildlife-oriented recreational development or protection of natural resources. It also authorizes the charging of fees for public uses.
Partnerships for Wildlife Act of 1992	Establishes a Wildlife Conservation and Appreciation Fund to receive appropriated funds and donations from the National Fish and Wildlife Foundation and other private sources to assist the state fish and game agencies in carrying out their responsibilities for conservation of non-game species. The funding formula is no more that 1/3 federal funds, at least 1/3 foundation funds, and at least 1/3 state funds.
Refuge Revenue Sharing Act of 1935, as amended	Provided for payments to counties in lieu of taxes from areas administered by the Fish and Wildlife Service. Counties are required to pass payments along to other units of local government within the county, which suffer losses in tax revenues due to the establishment of Service areas.
Rehabilitation Act of 1973	Requires nondiscrimination in the employment practices of federal agencies of the executive branch and contractors. It also requires all federally assisted programs, services, and activities to be available to people with disabilities.
Rivers and Harbors Appropriations Act of 1899, as amended	Requires the authorization by the U.S. Army Corps of Engineers prior to any work in, on, over, or under a navigable water of the United States. The Fish and Wildlife Coordination Act provides authority for the Service to review and comment on the effects on fish and wildlife activities proposed to be undertaken or permitted by the Corps of Engineers. Service concerns include contaminated sediments associated with dredge or fill projects in navigable waters.
Sikes Act (1960), as amended	Provides for the cooperation by the Departments of Interior and Defense with state agencies in planning, development, and maintenance of fish and wildlife resources and outdoor recreation facilities on military reservations throughout the United States. It requires the Secretary of each military department to use trained professionals to manage the wildlife and fishery resource under his jurisdiction, and requires that federal and state fish and wildlife agencies be given priority in management of fish and wildlife activities on military reservations.

STATUE	DESCRIPTION
Transfer of Certain Real Property for Wildlife Conservation Purposes Act of 1948	This Act provides that upon determination by the Administrator of the General Services Administration, real property no longer needed by a federal agency can be transferred, without reimbursement, to the Secretary of the Interior if the land has particular value for migratory birds, or to a state agency for other wildlife conservation purposes.
Transportation Equity Act for the 21st Century (1998)	Established the Refuge Roads Program, requires transportation planning that includes public involvement, and provides funding for approved public use roads and trails and associated parking lots, comfort stations, and bicycle/pedestrian facilities.
Uniform Relocation and Assistance and Real Property Acquisition Policies Act (1970), as amended	Provides for uniform and equitable treatment of persons who sell their homes, businesses, or farms to the Service. The Act requires that any purchase offer be no less than the fair market value of the property.
Water Resources Planning Act of 1965	Established Water Resources Council to be composed of Cabinet representatives including the Secretary of the Interior. The Council reviews river basin plans with respect to agricultural, urban, energy, industrial, recreational and fish and wildlife needs. The act also established a grant program to assist States in participating in the development of related comprehensive water and land use plans.
Wild and Scenic Rivers Act of 1968, as amended	This Act selects certain rivers of the nation possessing remarkable scenic, recreational, geologic, fish and wildlife, historic, cultural, or other similar values; preserves them in a free-flowing condition; and protects their local environments.
Wilderness Act of 1964, as amended	This Act directs the Secretary of the Interior to review every roadless area of 5,000 acres or more and every roadless island regardless of size within the National Wildlife Refuge System and to recommend suitability of each such area. The Act permits certain activities within designated wilderness areas that do not alter natural processes. Wilderness values are preserved through a "minimum tool" management approach, which requires refuge managers to use the least intrusive methods, equipment, and facilities necessary for administering the areas.
Youth Conservation Corps Act of 1970	Established a permanent Youth Conservation Corps (YCC) program within the Departments of Interior and Agriculture. Within the Service, YCC participants perform many tasks on refuges, fish hatcheries, and research stations.

EXECUTIVE ORDERS	DESCRIPTIONS
EO 11593, Protection and Enhancement of the Cultural Environment (1971)	States that if the Service proposes any development activities that may affect the archaeological or historic sites, the Service will consult with Federal and State Historic Preservation Officers to comply with Section 106 of the National Historic Preservation Act of 1966, as amended.
EO 11644, Use of Off-road Vehicles on Public Land (1972)	Established policies and procedures to ensure that the use of off-road vehicles on public lands will be controlled and directed so as to protect the resources of those lands, to promote the safety of all users of those lands, and to minimize conflicts among the various uses of those lands.
EO 11988, Floodplain Management (1977)	The purpose of this Executive Order is to prevent federal agencies from contributing to the "adverse impacts associated with occupancy and modification of floodplains" and the "direct or indirect support of floodplain development." In the course of fulfilling their respective authorities, federal agencies "shall take action to reduce the risk of flood loss, to minimize the impact of floods on human safety, health and welfare, and to restore and preserve the natural and beneficial values served by floodplains."
EO 11989 (1977), Amends Section 2 of EO 11644	Directs agencies to close areas negatively impacted by off-road vehicles.
EO 11990, Protection of Wetlands (1977)	Federal agencies are directed to provide leadership and take action to minimize the destruction, loss of degradation of wetlands, and to preserve and enhance the natural and beneficial values of wetlands.
EO 12372, Intergovernmental Review of Federal Programs (1982)	Seeks to foster intergovernmental partnerships by requiring federal agencies to use the state process to determine and address concerns of state and local elected officials with proposed federal assistance and development programs.
EO 12898, Environmental Justice (1994)	Requires federal agencies to identify and address disproportionately high and adverse effects of its programs, policies, and activities on minority and low-income populations.

EXECUTIVE ORDERS	DESCRIPTIONS
EO 12906, Coordinating Geographical Data Acquisition and Access (1994), Amended by EO 13286 (2003). Amendment of EOs and other actions in connection with transfer of certain functions to Secretary of DHS.	Recommended that the executive branch develop, in cooperation with state, local, and tribal governments, and the private sector, a coordinated National Spatial Data Infrastructure to support public and private sector applications of geospatial data. Of particular importance to comprehensive conservation planning is the National Vegetation Classification System (NVCS), which is the adopted standard for vegetation mapping. Using NVCS facilitates the compilation of regional and national summaries, which in turn, can provide an ecosystem context for individual refuges.
EO 12962, Recreational Fisheries (1995)	Federal agencies are directed to improve the quantity, function, sustainable productivity, and distribution of U.S. aquatic resources for increased recreational fishing opportunities in cooperation with states and tribes.
EO 13007, Native American Religious Practices (1996)	Provides for access to, and ceremonial use of, Indian sacred sites on federal lands used by Indian religious practitioners and direction to avoid adversely affecting the physical integrity of such sites.
EO 13061, Federal Support of Community Efforts Along American Heritage Rivers (1997)	Established the American Heritage Rivers initiative for the purpose of natural resource and environmental protection, economic revitalization, and historic and cultural preservation. The Act directs Federal agencies to preserve, protect, and restore rivers and their associated resources important to our history, culture, and natural heritage.
EO 13084, Consultation and Coordination With Indian Tribal Governments (2000)	Provides a mechanism for establishing regular and meaningful consultation and collaboration with tribal officials in the development of federal policies that have tribal implications.
EO 13112, Invasive Species (1999)	Federal agencies are directed to prevent the introduction of invasive species, detect and respond rapidly to and control populations of such species in a cost effective and environmentally sound manner, accurately monitor invasive species, provide for restoration of native species and habitat conditions, conduct research to prevent introductions and to control invasive species, and promote public education on invasive species and the means to address them. This EO replaces and rescinds EO 11987, Exotic Organisms (1977).

EXECUTIVE ORDERS	DESCRIPTIONS
EO 13186, Responsibilities of Federal Agencies to Protect Migratory Birds. (2001)	Instructs federal agencies to conserve migratory birds by several means, including the incorporation of strategies and recommendations found in Partners in Flight Bird Conservation plans, the North American Waterfowl Plan, the North American Waterbird Conservation Plan, and the United States Shorebird Conservation Plan, into agency management plans and guidance documents.

Appendix D. Public Involvement

SUMMARY OF PUBLIC SCOPING COMMENTS

November 2007

Refuges: Mandalay National Wildlife Refuge

Region: 4; Terrebonne, LA; Congressional District: Third

Background:

- Mandalay Established: May 2, 1996

- Located in state of Louisiana, Third Congressional District

- Mandalay NWR is 4,416 acres

- The purposes of Mandalay National Wildlife Refuge, based upon land acquisition documents and its establishing authority, are as follows:

  "... for use as an inviolate sanctuary, or for any other management purpose, for migratory birds.
  16 U.S.C. 715d (Migratory Bird Conservation Act).

  "... to conserve (A) fish or wildlife which are listed as endangered species or threatened species... or (B) plants..." 16 U.S.C. 1534 (Endangered Species Act of 1973).

- The Secretary of Louisiana Department of Wildlife and Fisheries (LDWF) was invited to participate in the planning process in November 2006, and LDWF personnel attended the Biological Reviews for Mandalay NWR in October 2006.

- Public involvement process:
  Public scoping was conducted through the following formal events-
  > Public Scoping Meeting - Houma, LA, April 10, 2007 (7 attended)

In addition to the meetings, fliers were placed in the local area and news releases were printed in the River Parishes Edition of the Times Picayune, the Houma Courier, the Daily Iberian, and the Franklin Banner-Tribune.

Issues from Public scoping meeting:

- Mandalay NWR:

Numerous comments were made requesting that the refuge remain open to hunting and fishing.

Improvement of refuge signage and outreach so the public can realize the great opportunity for outdoor experiences.

Introducing freshwater is important and needs to be addressed.

Continue and improve duck hunting by offering at least one blind in Lake Hatch and offering assistance with boat access by using Ducks Unlimited and volunteers.

Continue to offer deer hunting and nutria trapping.

The Director of Coastal Restoration and Preservation for Terrebonne Parish Consolidated Government made the following statements -

  o Funding for control of invasive species such as Chinese tallow and water hyacinth is a priority.

  o More staff is needed to effectively manage the refuge.

  o The partnership between Terrebonne Parish and the refuge is important in the areas of nutria control and restoration projects and should continue.

  o Bank stabilization is critical and sources such as Coastal Wetlands Planning and Protection and Restoration Act (CWPPRA) funds and grants should be used for supporting projects.

DRAFT PLAN COMMENTS AND SERVICE RESPONSES

This appendix summarizes all comments that were received on the Draft Comprehensive Conservation Plan and Environmental Impact Statement for Mandalay National Wildlife Refuge. Public comments on this draft document were accepted from May 28 to June 29, 2009.

A total of 11 individuals submitted comments on the Draft Comprehensive Conservation Plan and Environmental Assessment in writing. More than one individual represented some agencies or organizations.

AFFILIATIONS OF RESPONDENTS

The table below identifies the names and affiliations of respondents who commented on the Draft Comprehensive Conservation Plan and Environmental Assessment in writing or by telephone conversation. The refuge has close relationships with several state agencies, as well as non-governmental organizations that have been instrumental in protecting the lands of the Mandalay NWR and promoting ecotourism in the area.

Name of Respondent	Affiliation
Andy Ardoin	Louisiana Department of Wildlife and Fisheries – Baton Rouge, LA
Jean Public	Jean Public.com, Florham Park, NJ
Carol Crapanzano	Louisiana Department of Natural Resources – Baton Rouge, LA
William McGrath	Safari Club International – Washington, DC
Gregory DuCote	Louisiana Department of Natural Resources – Baton Rouge, LA
Timothy Allen	Apache Louisiana Minerals, LLC – Houma, LA
Scott Drapekin	Houma, LA
Ray Wolsefer	Hammond, LA
Claude Blanchard	Metairie, LA
April Hoover	NRA member – phone conversation
Ian Fry	frymap02@yahoo.com

The number of affiliations represented in the above table can be summarized as follows: state agencies (3); non-governmental organizations (2); general public (6).

COMMENT MEDIA

The types of media used to deliver the comments received by the refuge and planning staffs are categorized as follows: oral (1); written letter (4); and e-mail (6).

GEOGRAPHIC ORIGIN OF RESPONDENTS

The geographic origins of the individual respondents who submitted comments are Louisiana (7); New Jersey (1); Washington, DC (1); unknown (2).

SUMMARY OF CONCERNS AND THE SERVICE'S RESPONSES

The public comments received address the following concerns. The Service's responses to each concern are also summarized.

HABITATS – FIRE

Comment: Ban all prescribed fires.

Service Response: There are no plans to include prescribed fire as a management tool at Mandalay NWR in the immediate future. A fire management step-down plan is scheduled for completion in 2009.

VISITOR SERVICES (PUBLIC USE) – OPPOSITION TO HUNTING

Comment: Eliminate hunting on the refuge. (2 comments)

Service Response: Hunting is one of the six priority public uses of the Refuge System as specified in the Improvement Act. The Service allows hunting as long as it is compatible with the mission of the Service, the Refuge System, and the purposes of the refuge.

VISITOR SERVICES (PUBLIC USE) – HUNTING

Comment: Please continue hunting programs on the refuge, including youth hunt programs (5 comments).

Service Response: Comment noted. Hunting is one of the six priority public uses of the Refuge System as specified in the Improvement Act. The Service allows hunting as long as it is compatible with the mission of the Service, the Refuge System, and the purposes of the refuge.

Comment: Please continue hunting programs on the refuge, but do not increase hunting opportunities (1 comment).

Service Response: Comment noted. Hunting is one of the six priority public uses of the Refuge System as specified in the Improvement Act. The Service allows hunting as long as it is compatible with the mission of the Service, the Refuge System, and the purposes of the refuge. The current hunting program on Mandalay NWR has been deemed compatible.

RESOURCE PROTECTION- MANAGEMENT DIRECTION

Comment: We have no substantive changes or comments regarding the management direction or plan implementation.

Service Response: Comment noted.

Comment: Activity is consistent with the Louisiana Coastal Resource Program.

Service Response: Comment noted.

States' Position on the Preferred Alternative and Our Response: The Louisiana Department of Wildlife and Fisheries (LDWF) participated in the CCP process as a member of the core planning team. LDWF reviewed the internal and draft CCPs. Comments during the internal review regarding editorial changes were incorporated into the draft CCP. LDWF supports the goals and strategies of the CCP.

Appendix E. Appropriate Use Determinations

Appropriate Use Determinations

An appropriate use determination is the initial decision process a refuge manager follows when first considering whether or not to allow a proposed use on a refuge. The refuge manager must find a use is appropriate before undertaking a compatibility review of the use. This process clarifies and expands on the compatibility determination process, by describing when refuge managers should deny a proposed use without determining compatibility. If we find a proposed use is not appropriate, we will not allow the use and will not prepare a compatibility determination.

Except for the uses noted below, the refuge manager must decide if a new or existing use is an appropriate refuge use. If an existing use is not appropriate, the refuge manager will eliminate or modify the use as expeditiously as practicable. If a new use is not appropriate, the refuge manager will deny the use without determining compatibility. Uses that have been administratively determined to be appropriate are:

- Six wildlife-dependent recreational uses - As defined by the National Wildlife Refuge System Improvement Act of 1997 (Improvement Act), the six wildlife-dependent recreational uses (hunting, fishing, wildlife observation, wildlife photography, and environmental education and interpretation) are determined to be appropriate. However, the refuge manager must still determine if these uses are compatible.

- Take of fish and wildlife under State regulations - States have regulations concerning take of wildlife that includes hunting, fishing, and trapping. We consider take of wildlife under such regulations appropriate. However, the refuge manager must determine if the activity is compatible before allowing it on a refuge.

Statutory Authorities for this policy:

National Wildlife Refuge System Administration Act of 1966, as amended by the National Wildlife Refuge System Improvement Act of 1997, 16 U.S.C. 668dd-668ee (Administration Act). This law provides the authority for establishing policies and regulations governing refuge uses, including the authority to prohibit certain harmful activities. The Administration Act does not authorize any particular use, but rather authorizes the Secretary of the Interior to allow uses only when they are compatible and "under such regulations as he may prescribe." This law specifically identifies certain public uses that, when compatible, are legitimate and appropriate uses within the Refuge System. The law states ". . . it is the policy of the United States that . . .compatible wildlife-dependent recreation is a legitimate and appropriate general public use of the System . . . .compatible wildlife-dependent recreational uses are the priority general public uses of the System and shall receive priority consideration in refuge planning and management; and . . . when the Secretary determines that a proposed wildlife-dependent recreational use is a compatible use within a refuge, that activity should be facilitated . . . the Secretary shall . . . ensure that priority general public uses of the System receive enhanced consideration over other general public uses in planning and management within the System . . . ." The law also states "in administering the System, the Secretary is authorized to take the following actions: . . . issue regulations to carry out this Act." This policy implements the standards set in the Administration Act by providing enhanced consideration of priority general public uses and ensuring other public uses do not interfere with our ability to provide quality, wildlife-dependent recreational uses.

Refuge Recreation Act of 1962, 16 U.S.C. 460k (Recreation Act). This law authorizes the Secretary of the Interior to ". . . administer such areas [of the System] or parts thereof for public recreation when in his judgment public recreation can be an appropriate incidental or secondary use." While the Recreation Act authorizes us to allow public recreation in areas of the Refuge System when the use is an "appropriate incidental or secondary use," the Improvement Act provides the Refuge System mission and includes specific directives and a clear hierarchy of public uses on the Refuge System.

Other Statutes that Establish Refuges, including the Alaska National Interest Lands Conservation Act of 1980 (ANILCA) (16 U.S.C. 410hh - 410hh-5, 460 mm - 460mm-4, 539-539e, and 3101 - 3233; 43 U.S.C. 1631 et seq.).

Executive Orders. We must comply with Executive Order (E.O.) 11644 when allowing use of off-highway vehicles on refuges. This order requires that we: designate areas as open or closed to off-highway vehicles in order to protect refuge resources, promote safety, and minimize conflict among the various refuge users; monitor the effects of these uses once they are allowed; and amend or rescind any area designation as necessary based on the information gathered. Furthermore, E.O. 11989 requires us to close areas to off highway vehicles when we determine that the use causes or will cause considerable adverse effects on the soil, vegetation, wildlife, habitat, or cultural or historic resources. Statutes, such as ANILCA, take precedence over executive orders.

Definitions:

Appropriate Use
A proposed or existing use on a refuge that meets at least one of the following four conditions.

1) The use is a wildlife-dependent recreational use as identified in the Improvement Act.
2) The use contributes to fulfilling the refuge purpose(s), the Refuge System mission, or goals or objectives described in a refuge management plan approved after October 9, 1997, the date the Improvement Act was signed into law.
3) The use involves the take of fish and wildlife under State regulations.
4) The use has been found to be appropriate as specified in section 1.11.

Native American. American Indians in the conterminous United States and Alaska Natives (including Aleuts, Eskimos, and Indians) who are members of federally recognized tribes.

Priority General Public Use. A compatible wildlife-dependent recreational use of a refuge involving hunting, fishing, wildlife observation, wildlife photography, and environmental education and interpretation.

Quality. The criteria used to determine a quality recreational experience include:

- Promotes safety of participants, other visitors, and facilities.
- Promotes compliance with applicable laws and regulations and responsible behavior.
- Minimizes or eliminates conflicts with fish and wildlife population or habitat goals or objectives in a plan approved after 1997.
- Minimizes or eliminates conflicts with other compatible wildlife-dependent recreation.
- Minimizes conflicts with neighboring landowners.
- Promotes accessibility and availability to a broad spectrum of the American people.
- Promotes resource stewardship and conservation.
- Promotes public understanding and increases public appreciation of America's natural resources and our role in managing and protecting these resources.
- Provides reliable/reasonable opportunities to experience wildlife.
- Uses facilities that are accessible and blend into the natural setting.
- Uses visitor satisfaction to help define and evaluate programs.

Wildlife-Dependent Recreational Use. As defined by the Improvement Act, a use of a refuge involving hunting, fishing, wildlife observation, wildlife photography, and environmental education and interpretation.

FINDING OF APPROPRIATENESS OF A REFUGE USE

Refuge Name: Mandalay National Wildlife Refuge
Use: Boating

This form is not required for wildlife-dependent recreational uses, take regulated by the State, or uses already described in a refuge CCP or step-down management plan approved after October 9, 1997.

Decision Criteria:	YES	NO
(a) Do we have jurisdiction over the use?	X	
(b) Does the use comply with applicable laws and regulations (Federal, State, tribal, and local)?	X	
(c) Is the use consistent with applicable executive orders and Department and Service policies?	X	
(d) Is the use consistent with public safety?	X	
(e) Is the use consistent with goals and objectives in an approved management plan or other document?	X	
(f) Has an earlier documented analysis not denied the use or is this the first time the use has been proposed?	X	
(g) Is the use manageable within available budget and staff?	X	
(h) Will this be manageable in the future within existing resources?	X	
(i) Does the use contribute to the public's understanding and appreciation of the refuge's natural or cultural resources, or is the use beneficial to the refuge's natural or cultural resources?	X	
(j) Can the use be accommodated without impairing existing wildlife-dependent recreational uses or reducing the potential to provide quality (see section 1.6D, 603 FW 1, for description), compatible, wildlife-dependent recreation into the future?	X	

Where we do not have jurisdiction over the use ["no" to (a)], there is no need to evaluate it further as we cannot control the use. Uses that are illegal, inconsistent with existing policy, or unsafe ["no" to (b), (c), or (d)] may not be found appropriate. If the answer is "no" to any of the other questions above, we will **generally** not allow the use.

If indicated, the refuge manager has consulted with State fish and wildlife agencies.   **Yes ___ No __X_**

When the refuge manager finds the use appropriate based on sound professional judgment, the refuge manager must justify the use in writing on an attached sheet and obtain the refuge supervisor's concurrence.

Based on an overall assessment of these factors, my summary conclusion is that the proposed use is:

Not Appropriate_____   Appropriate__X___

Refuge Manager:_____   Date:___8-6-09_____

If found to be **Not Appropriate**, the refuge supervisor does not need to sign concurrence if the use is a new use. If an existing use is found **Not Appropriate** outside the CCP process, the refuge supervisor must sign concurrence. If found to be **Appropriate**, the refuge supervisor must sign concurrence.

Refuge Supervisor:_____   Date:__8-17-09_____
A compatibility determination is required before the use may be allowed.

FINDING OF APPROPRIATENESS OF A REFUGE USE

Refuge Name: Mandalay National Wildlife Refuge

Use: Control of Mammals (nutria) and alligators

This form is not required for wildlife-dependent recreational uses, take regulated by the State, or uses already described in a refuge CCP or step-down management plan approved after October 9, 1997.

Decision Criteria:	YES	NO
(a) Do we have jurisdiction over the use?	X	
(b) Does the use comply with applicable laws and regulations (Federal, State, tribal, and local)?	X	
(c) Is the use consistent with applicable executive orders and Department and Service policies?	X	
(d) Is the use consistent with public safety?	X	
(e) Is the use consistent with goals and objectives in an approved management plan or other document?	X	
(f) Has an earlier documented analysis not denied the use or is this the first time the use has been proposed?	X	
(g) Is the use manageable within available budget and staff?	X	
(h) Will this be manageable in the future within existing resources?	X	
(i) Does the use contribute to the public's understanding and appreciation of the refuge's natural or cultural resources, or is the use beneficial to the refuge's natural or cultural resources?	X	
(j) Can the use be accommodated without impairing existing wildlife-dependent recreational uses or reducing the potential to provide quality (see section 1.6D, 603 FW 1, for description), compatible, wildlife-dependent recreation into the future?	X	

Where we do not have jurisdiction over the use ["no" to (a)], there is no need to evaluate it further as we cannot control the use. Uses that are illegal, inconsistent with existing policy, or unsafe ["no" to (b), (c), or (d)] may not be found appropriate. If the answer is "no" to any of the other questions above, we will **generally** not allow the use.

If indicated, the refuge manager has consulted with State fish and wildlife agencies. Yes __X_   No ___

When the refuge manager finds the use appropriate based on sound professional judgment, the refuge manager must justify the use in writing on an attached sheet and obtain the refuge supervisor's concurrence.

Based on an overall assessment of these factors, my summary conclusion is that the proposed use is:

Not Appropriate _____   Appropriate __X___

Refuge Manager: _____   Date: 8-6-09

If found to be **Not Appropriate**, the refuge supervisor does not need to sign concurrence if the use is a new use. If an existing use is found **Not Appropriate** outside the CCP process, the refuge supervisor must sign concurrence. If found to be **Appropriate**, the refuge supervisor must sign concurrence.

Refuge Supervisor: _____   Date: 8-9-09

A compatibility determination is required before the use may be allowed.

Appendix F. Compatibility Determinations

Compatibility Determination

Uses: The following uses were considered for compatibility determination:

1) Boating in accordance with U.S. Coast Guard and the State of Louisiana regulations
2) Recreational fishing of freshwater and saltwater fish in accordance with State of Louisiana regulations
3) Recreational hunting of migratory birds, big-game, and feral hogs in accordance with the State of Louisiana regulations
4) Wildlife observation/photography
5) Control of mammals (nutria) and alligators
6) Environmental education and interpretation

A description and the anticipated biological impacts for each are addressed separately in this Compatibility Determination.

Refuge Name: Mandalay National Wildlife Refuge.

Date Established: May 2, 1996

Establishing and Acquisition Authorities: Migratory bird Conservation Act of 1929 and Endangered Species Act of 1973.

Refuge Purpose: The purposes of the refuge are: "…for use as an inviolate sanctuary, or for any other management purpose, for migratory birds." 16 U.S.C. 715d (Migratory Bird Conservation Act)

"…to conserve (A) fish or wildlife which are listed as endangered species or threatened species…or (B) plants…" 16 U.S.C. 1534 (Endangered Species Act of 1973)

National Wildlife Refuge System Mission:

The mission of the Refuge System, as defined by the National Wildlife Refuge System Improvement Act of 1997, is:

> … to administer a national network of lands and waters for the conservation, management, and where appropriate, restoration of the fish, wildlife and plant resources and their habitats within the United States for the benefit of present and future generations of Americans.

Other Applicable Laws, Regulations, and Policies:

Antiquities Act of 1906 (34 Stat. 225)
Migratory Bird Treaty Act of 1918 (15 U.S.C. 703-711; 40 Stat. 755)
Migratory Bird Conservation Act of 1929 (16 U.S.C. 715r; 45 Stat. 1222)
Migratory Bird Hunting Stamp Act of 1934 (16 U.S.C. 718-178h; 48 Stat. 451)
Criminal Code Provisions of 1940 (18 U.S.C. 41)
Bald and Golden Eagle Protection Act (16 U.S.C. 668-668d; 54 Stat. 250)

Refuge Trespass Act of June 25, 1948 (18 U.S.C. 41; 62 Stat. 686)
Fish and Wildlife Act of 1956 (16 U.S.C. 742a-742j; 70 Stat.1119)
Refuge Recreation Act of 1962 (16 U.S.C. 460k-460k-4; 76 Stat. 653)
Wilderness Act (16 U.S.C. 1131; 78 Stat. 890)
Land and Water Conservation Fund Act of 1965
National Historic Preservation Act of 1966, as amended (16 U.S.C. 470, et seq.; 80 Stat. 915)
National Wildlife Refuge System Administration Act of 1966 (16 U.S.C. 668dd, 668ee; 80 Stat. 927)
National Environmental Policy Act of 1969, NEPA (42 U.S.C. 4321, et seq; 83 Stat. 852)
Use of Off-Road Vehicles on Public Lands (Executive Order 11644, as amended by
Executive Order 10989)
Endangered Species Act of 1973 (16 U.S.C. 1531 et seq; 87 Stat. 884)
Refuge Revenue Sharing Act of 1935, as amended in 1978 (16 U.S.C. 715s; 92 Stat. 1319)
National Wildlife Refuge Regulations for the Most Recent Fiscal Year
(50 CFR Subchapter C; 43 CFR 3101.3-3)
Emergency Wetlands Resources Act of 1986 (S.B. 740)
North American Wetlands Conservation Act of 1990
Food Security Act (Farm Bill) of 1990 as amended (HR 2100)
The Property Clause of The U.S. Constitution Article IV 3, Clause 2
The Commerce Clause of The U.S. Constitution Article 1, Section 8
The National Wildlife Refuge System Improvement Act of 1997 (Public Law 105-57, USC668dd)
Executive Order 12996, Management and General public Use of the National Wildlife Refuge
System. March 25, 1996
Title 50, Code of Federal Regulations, Parts 25-33
Archaeological Resources Protection Act of 1979
Native American Graves Protection and Repatriation Act of 1990
National Wildlife Refuge System Improvement Act of 1997 (Public law 105-57, October 9, 1997)

Compatibility determinations for each description listed are considered separately. Although, for brevity, the preceding sections from "Uses" through "Other Applicable Laws, Regulations and Policies" are only written once within the CCP, they are part of each descriptive use and become part of that compatibility determination if considered outside of the CCP.

Description of Use: Boating (motorized and non-motorized)

This use involves recreational boating over and adjacent to refuge-owned water bottoms. These uses are hunting, fishing, wildlife observation, and wildlife photography. No air boats are allowed on refuge waters without a permit.

Availability of Resources: Funding for boating is supported by annual operation and maintenance funds. Costs include permit printing, administration, and monitoring the activity.

Anticipated Impacts of the Use: Boating use whether it is motorized or non-motorized over refuge waters for regulated public use activities in accordance with permit regulations should not have any significant adverse biological impacts. As currently proposed, the known and anticipated levels of disturbance of allowing boating fishing is considered minimal and well within the tolerance level of known fish and wildlife species and populations present on the refuge. Implementation of an effective law enforcement program and development of site-specific refuge regulations that are reviewed annually should minimize most problems.

Public Review and Comment: The public review comment period was from May 28 to June 29, 2009. Methods used to solicit public review and comment included posted notices at refuge headquarters and area locations; copies of the draft comprehensive conservation plan distributed to adjacent landowners, the public, and local, state, and federal agencies; news releases sent to the local area newspaper (Houma Courier). Appendix D summarizes the public comments.

Determination (check one below):

_____ Use is Not Compatible

__X__ Use is Compatible with Following Stipulations

Stipulations Necessary to Ensure Compatibility:

- Air boats are prohibited on the refuge waters.

Justification: The National Wildlife Refuge System Improvement Act of 1997 identified hunting, fishing, wildlife observation, and wildlife photography as priority public uses on national wildlife refuges, where compatible with refuge purposes. Boat access is the only access available to the refuge due to its remote location. This use is legitimate and appropriate. Offering recreational boating is in compliance with refuge goals, is a management objective for Mandalay National Wildlife Refuge, and furthers the goals and missions of the National Wildlife Refuge System.

NEPA Compliance for Refuge Use Description: *Place an X in appropriate space.*

_____Categorical Exclusion without Environmental Action Statement
_____Categorical Exclusion and Environmental Action Statement
___X___Environmental Assessment and Finding of No Significant Impact
_____Environmental Impact Statement and Record of Decision

Mandatory 10-year Re-evaluation Date: 09/14/2019

(2) Description of Use: Recreational Fishing

Recreational fishing, a wildlife-dependent activity, has been identified in the National Wildlife Refuge System Improvement Act of 1997 as a priority public use, provided it is compatible with the purpose for which the refuge was established.

Recreational fishing of freshwater and saltwater species is allowed year-round on the refuge. While fishing is a popular public use on the refuge, fishing pressure is not heavy at this time.
All fishing falls within the framework of Louisiana's open seasons and follows state regulations. Refuge-specific regulations are reviewed annually and incorporated into the refuge hunting and fishing brochure. Fishermen are not required to possess refuge permits while fishing on the refuge. The entire refuge is open to fishing during hours of daylight with the exception of areas posted with "Area Closed" signs or so designated in the hunting and fishing permit during state waterfowl seasons.

Limb lines, trotlines, slat traps, nets, are prohibited. Jug lines are allowed but must be attended and not left overnight. No commercial fishing activities, including guiding or participating in a charter fishing trip, are permitted.

Availability of Resources: Funding for the fishing program is supported by annual operation and maintenance funds. Costs include administration and monitoring the activity.

Anticipated Impacts of the Use: While managed fishing opportunities result in both short- and long-term impacts to individual fish, effects at the population level are usually negligible. The fish populations are capable of sustaining harvest because of the availability of excellent habitat. Fishing regulations for both saltwater and freshwater species are based on specific state-wide harvest objectives. State biologists set limits and harvest guidelines based on population surveys and habitat condition data. Refuge fishing programs are always within these regulations. As currently proposed, the known and anticipated levels of disturbance by allowing fishing is considered minimal and well within the tolerance level of known fish species and populations present on the refuge. All fishing activities would be conducted with the constraints of sound biological principles and refuge-specific regulations established to restrict illegal or questionable activities. Monitoring activities through fish inventories in partnerships with the state and assessments of public use levels and activities and public use programs would be adjusted as needed to limit disturbance. Implementation of an effective law enforcement program and development of site-specific refuge regulations that are reviewed annually should minimize most problems.

Public Review and Comment: The public review comment period was from May 28 to June 29, 2009. Methods used to solicit public review and comment included posted notices at refuge headquarters and area locations; copies of the draft comprehensive conservation plan distributed to adjacent landowners, the public, and local, state, and federal agencies; news releases sent to the local area newspaper (Houma Courier). Appendix D summarizes the public comments.

Determination (check one below):

_____ Use is Not Compatible

__X__ Use is Compatible with Following Stipulations

Stipulations Necessary to Ensure Compatibility:

- Fishing is allowed in accordance with state established annual regulations and limits as set by Louisiana Department of Wildlife and Fisheries.
- Sport fishing is permitted only during daylight hours.
- Limb lines, trotlines, slat traps, and nets are prohibited.

Justification: The National Wildlife Refuge System Improvement Act of 1997 identified fishing as one of the priority public uses on national wildlife refuges, where compatible with refuge purposes. This use is legitimate and appropriate and is dependent upon healthy fish populations. Offering fishing is in compliance with refuge goals, is a management objective for Mandalay National Wildlife Refuge, and furthers the goals and missions of the National Wildlife Refuge System.

NEPA Compliance for Refuge Use Description: *Place an X in appropriate space.*

_____Categorical Exclusion without Environmental Action Statement
_____Categorical Exclusion and Environmental Action Statement
___X___Environmental Assessment and Finding of No Significant Impact
_____Environmental Impact Statement and Record of Decision

Mandatory 15-year Re-evaluation Date: 09/14/2024

(3) Description of Use: Recreational Hunting

Recreational hunting, a wildlife-dependent activity, has been identified in the National Wildlife Refuge System Improvement Act of 1997 as a priority public use, provided it is compatible with the purpose for which the refuge was established, and Executive Order 13443, Facilitation of Hunting Heritage and Wildlife Conservation, dated August 17, 2007. The order directs federal agencies that have programs and activities that have a measurable effect on public land management, outdoor recreation, and wildlife management, including the Departments of Interior and Agriculture, to facilitate the expansion and enhancement of hunting opportunities and the management of game species and their habitat.

Recreational hunting of white-tailed deer with bow and arrow is allowed on the refuge. Hunters are also allowed to take feral hogs with bow and arrow during archery deer season. All hunts fall within the framework of Louisiana's open seasons and follow state regulations. Refuge-specific regulations are reviewed annually and incorporated into the refuge hunting permit. Hunters are required to possess refuge permits while hunting on the refuge. The entire refuge is open to hunting.

Waterfowl (ducks and geese), coots, rails, and gallinules may be hunted by lottery permit during the state season on Wednesday, and on Saturday until noon, using non-toxic shot. Retrievers are allowed. White-tailed deer harvest is limited to archery only during the state season. State bag limits and regulations will be adopted on the refuge. No commercial hunting activities, including guiding or participating in a guided hunt, are permitted. Harvest information is gathered by mandatory self-check form contained in the hunting permit that is deposited daily in check station boxes on the refuge.

Availability of Resources: Funding for the hunt program is supported by annual operation and maintenance funds. Costs include permit printing, administration, and monitoring the activity.

Anticipated Impacts of the Use: While managed hunting opportunities result in take of some individual animals, short-term impacts to individual animals at the population level are usually negligible. Hunting regulations for both endemic and migratory game species are based on specific state-wide and nation-wide harvest objectives. Migratory bird regulations are established at the federal level each year following a series of meetings involving both state and federal biologists. Harvest guidelines are based on population survey and habitat condition data. Refuge hunting programs are always within these regulations. As currently proposed, the known and anticipated levels of disturbance of allowing hunting are considered minimal and well within the tolerance level of known wildlife species and populations present on the refuge. All hunting activities would be conducted with the constraints of sound biological principles and refuge-specific regulations established to restrict illegal or questionable activities. Monitoring activities through wildlife inventories and assessments of public use levels and activities would be utilized, and public use programs would be adjusted as needed to limit disturbance. Implementation of an effective law enforcement program and development of site specific refuge regulations that are reviewed annually should minimize most incidental take problems.

Public Review and Comment: The public review comment period was from May 28 to June 29, 2009. Methods used to solicit public review and comment included posted notices at refuge headquarters and area locations; copies of the draft comprehensive conservation plan distributed to adjacent landowners, the public, and local, state, and federal agencies; news releases sent to the local area newspaper (Houma Courier). Appendix D summarizes the public comments.

Determination (check one below):

_____ Use is Not Compatible

__X__ Use is Compatible with Following Stipulations

Stipulations Necessary to Ensure Compatibility:

- Hunting seasons and bag limits are established annually as agreed upon during the annual hunt coordination meeting with Louisiana Department of Wildlife and Fisheries personnel.
- All hunters are required to possess a signed refuge hunting permit while participating in refuge hunts. State hunting regulations apply unless otherwise listed in the permit.
- Non-toxic shot must be used.

Justification: The National Wildlife Refuge System Improvement Act of 1997 identified hunting as one of the priority public uses on national wildlife refuges, where compatible with refuge purposes. Executive Order 13443, Facilitation of Hunting Heritage and Wildlife Conservation, dated August 17, 2007, directs federal agencies that have programs and activities that have a measurable effect on public land management, outdoor recreation, and wildlife management, including the Departments of Interior and Agriculture, to facilitate the expansion and enhancement of hunting opportunities and the management of game species and their habitat.

This use is legitimate and appropriate and is dependent upon healthy wildlife populations. Offering hunting is in compliance with refuge goals, is a management objective for Mandalay National Wildlife Refuge, and furthers the goals and missions of the National Wildlife Refuge System.

NEPA Compliance for Refuge Use Description: *Place an X in appropriate space.*

_____Categorical Exclusion without Environmental Action Statement
_____Categorical Exclusion and Environmental Action Statement
___X___Environmental Assessment and Finding of No Significant Impact
_____Environmental Impact Statement and Record of Decision

Mandatory 15-year Re-evaluation Date: 09/14/2024

(4) Description of Use: Wildlife Observation and Photography

Wildlife observation and photography have been identified in the National Wildlife Refuge System Improvement Act of 1997 as priority wildlife-dependent recreation uses provided they are compatible with the purpose for which the refuge was established.

Though photography and observation have occurred on the refuge, there is an observation platform located on the terminus of the Mandalay National Wildlife Refuge nature trail designated for these activities. However, opportunity exists for visitors traveling to the refuge by boat for these activities. Commercial photography or videography is allowed under a special use permit with conditions specific to those activities. Often copies of photos or videos are given to the refuge for use with specific programs or publications.

The general public may participate in wildlife observation and photography year-round from one half hour before sunrise to one half hour after sunset in the open areas of the refuge. Boating is the only available access available for these activities except that on the nature trail mentioned above.

Availability of Resources: Funding for wildlife observation and photography use is supported by annual operation and maintenance funds. Costs include administering and monitoring the activity.

Anticipated Impacts of the Use: Wildlife observation and photography should not have any significant adverse biological impacts. As currently proposed, the known and anticipated levels of disturbance of allowing these activities is considered minimal and well within the tolerance level of known fish and wildlife species and populations present on the refuge. Implementation of an effective law enforcement program and development of site-specific refuge regulations that are reviewed annually should minimize most problems.

Public Review and Comment: The public review comment period was from May 28 to June 29, 2009. Methods used to solicit public review and comment included posted notices at refuge headquarters and area locations; copies of the draft comprehensive conservation plan distributed to adjacent landowners, the public, and local, state, and federal agencies; news releases sent to the local area newspaper (Houma Courier). Appendix D summarizes the public comments.

Determination (check one below):

_____ Use is Not Compatible

__X__ Use is Compatible with Following Stipulations

Stipulations Necessary to Ensure Compatibility:

- The refuge is open 30 minutes before legal sunrise to 30 minutes after legal sunset for all public use on the refuge.

Justification: The National Wildlife Refuge System Improvement Act of 1997 identified wildlife observation and wildlife photography as two of the priority public uses on national wildlife refuges, where compatible with refuge purposes. This use is legitimate and appropriate and is dependent upon healthy wildlife populations. Offering wildlife observation and wildlife photography is in compliance with refuge goals, is a management objective for Mandalay National Wildlife Refuge, and furthers the goals and missions of the National Wildlife Refuge System.

NEPA Compliance for Refuge Use Description: *Place an X in appropriate space.*

_____Categorical Exclusion without Environmental Action Statement
_____Categorical Exclusion and Environmental Action Statement
___X___Environmental Assessment and Finding of No Significant Impact
_____Environmental Impact Statement and Record of Decision

Mandatory 15-year Re-evaluation Date: 09/14/2024

(5) Description of Use: Control of nutria and alligators (Trapping**)**

Trapping is employed to prevent or reduce habitat damage and targets nutria, an exotic species native to South America, which was imported by fur farms in the early 1900s. When the fur farming industry collapsed after World War II, many were released or were not recaptured after escaping. The descendants established themselves in the marshes and have adapted well to the Louisiana coastal zone.

Since nutria are almost exclusively vegetarians, and can eat nearly 4 pounds of food daily, they can be very detrimental to marsh vegetation. Their burrows can also damage levees and banks. They are in direct competition with the native muskrat for habitat and food. Trapping nutria would be allowed by special use permits that designate locations and methods for their removal. Trappers participate in the Coast Wide Nutria Control Program, which is administered by the Louisiana Department of Wildlife and Fisheries.

Alligator harvest is employed to maintain control of a very robust alligator population on the refuge. An annual night count of alligators is conducted and this count has ranged from 700 to more than 1,200 alligators. Trappers are selected by a lottery drawing every 3 years. The refuge adopts state regulations for alligator harvest.

Availability of Resources: Funding for use is supported by annual operation and maintenance funds. Costs include administration and monitoring the activity.

Anticipated Impacts of the Use: The special use permit system allows the refuge manager to specifically regulate locations and methods for nutria removal and alligator harvest. Areas will be well marked and traps/lines will not be set in areas with high use by other visitors. Disturbance to non-target wildlife will be occasional, temporary, and isolated to small geographic areas. Positive impacts for nutria will be the control of an exotic species and reducing damage to refuge resources. Positive impacts for alligators will be population control and visitor safety.

Public Review and Comment: The public review comment period was from May 28 to June 29, 2009. Methods used to solicit public review and comment included posted notices at refuge headquarters and area locations; copies of the draft comprehensive conservation plan distributed to adjacent landowners, the public, and local, state, and federal agencies; news releases sent to the local area newspaper (Houma Courier). Appendix D summarizes the public comments.

Determination (check one below):

_____ Use is Not Compatible

__X__ Use is Compatible with Following Stipulations

Stipulations Necessary to Ensure Compatibility:

- Trapping is conducted in compliance with a special use permit.
- Trapping will not be allowed in high-use public areas.
- Take of non-target animals will be minimized by trap set and locations.
- A trapping report will be required of the individual named in the special use permit.
- All traps must be well marked and checked daily.

Justification: Trapping is a valuable management tool that is used to prevent and reduce damage to refuge habitat by nutria. With the above stipulations, little to no adverse effects to other refuge programs or wildlife species will occur. This use is in compliance with the Comprehensive Conservation Plan and furthers the goals and missions of the National Wildlife Refuge System and the refuge.

NEPA Compliance for Refuge Use Description: *Place an X in appropriate space.*

_____Categorical Exclusion without Environmental Action Statement
_____Categorical Exclusion and Environmental Action Statement
___X___Environmental Assessment and Finding of No Significant Impact
_____Environmental Impact Statement and Record of Decision

Mandatory 10-year Re-evaluation Date: 09/14/2019

(6) Description of Use: Environmental Education and Interpretation

Environmental education and interpretation have been identified in the National Wildlife Refuge System Improvement Act of 1997 as priority wildlife-dependent recreation uses provided they are compatible with the purpose for which the refuge was established.

Kiosks play a key role in environmental education and interpretation at the refuge. Additional information panels will be placed at all key public use facilities and access areas. In response to visitors' requests, the refuge will create additional informative and useful brochures highlighting the refuge, species lists, wildlife facts, and habitats.

Staff members participate in local community events by providing displays or setting up booths at local festivals, fairs, and boat shows. Refuge displays highlight the Fish and Wildlife Service, the National Wildlife Refuge System, and the refuge and its wildlife and habitats.

Availability of Resources: At the current participation level for this use, resources are adequate. However, with implementation of the preferred alternative, use will increase and additional resources will be required.

Anticipated Impacts of Use: The incidental disturbance of wildlife species, either illegally or unintentionally, may occur with any public use program. Environmental education and interpretation may result in some additional wildlife disturbance. Habitat destruction (mostly trampling) by approved or unapproved activity may also occur. Boardwalks, kiosks, and observation platforms are designed and placed to minimize disturbance potential. Effective education and law enforcement programs should minimize this disturbance factor.

Environmental education and interpretation are not expected to negatively impact refuge resources even though there may be some minimal and direct short-term disturbance or trampling.

Public Review and Comment: The public review comment period was from May 28 to June 29, 2009. Methods used to solicit public review and comment included posted notices at refuge headquarters and area locations; copies of the draft comprehensive conservation plan distributed to adjacent landowners, the public, and local, state, and federal agencies; news releases sent to the local area newspaper (Houma Courier). Appendix D summarizes the public comments.

Determination (check one below):

_____ Use is Not Compatible

___X___ Use is Compatible with the Following Stipulations

Stipulations Necessary to Ensure Compatibility: N/A

Justification: According to the National Wildlife Refuge System Improvement Act of 1997, environmental education and interpretation are priority public use activities that should be encouraged and expanded where possible. It is through compatible public uses such as these that the public becomes aware of and provides support for national wildlife refuges.

NEPA Compliance for Refuge Use Decision: *Place an X in appropriate space.*

_____Categorical Exclusion without Environmental Action Statement
_____Categorical Exclusion and Environmental Action Statement
___X___Environmental Assessment and Finding of No Significant Impact
_____Environmental Impact Statement and Record of Decision

Mandatory 15-Year Re-Evaluation Date: 09/14/2024

Approval of Compatibility Determinations

The signature of approval is for all compatibility determinations considered within the Comprehensive Conservation Plan for Mandalay National Wildlife Refuge. If one of the descriptive uses is considered for compatibility outside of the Comprehensive Conservation Plan, the approval signature becomes part of that determination.

Refuge Manager: _____ 8-05-09 _____

(Signature/Date)

Regional Compatibility Coordinator: _____ 09-09-09 _____

(Signature/Date)

Refuge Supervisor: _____ 8-17-09 _____

(Signature/Date)

Regional Chief, National Wildlife Refuge System, Southeast Region: _____ 9/11/09 _____

(Signature/Date)

Appendix G. Intra-Service Section 7 Biological Evaluation

Not Applicable for Mandalay NWR.

Appendix H. Refuge Biota

Species of concern and/or significance for management purposes occurring on Mandalay National Wildlife Refuge are listed below. For a complete list of birds found on the refuges, contact refuge headquarters for a bird list.

Mandalay National Wildlife Refuge

Common Name	Scientific Name
Birds	
Bald Eagle	Haliaeetus leucocephalus
Eastern Brown Pelican	Pelecanus occidentalis carolinensis
Wood Duck	Aix sponsa
Gadwall	Anas strepera
American Widgeon	Anas americana
Mallard	Anas platyrhynvchos
Mottled Duck	Anas fulvigula
Blue-winged Teal	Anas discors
Northern Shoveler	Anas clypeata
Northern Pintail	Anas acuta
Green-winged Teal	Anas crecca
Canvasback	Aytha valisineria
Redhead	Aythya americana
Ring-necked Duck	Aythya collaris
Greater Scaup	Aythya marila
Lesser Scaup	Aythya affinis
Common Goldeneye	Bucephala clangula
Bufflehead	Bucephala albeola
Hooded Merganser	Lophodytes cucullatus
Red-breasted Merganser	Mergus serrator
Ruddy Duck	Oxyura jamaicensis
Black-bellied whistling Duck	Dendrocygna autumnalis
Osprey	Pandion heliaetus
King Rail	Rallus elegans
Clapper Rail	Rallus longirostris
Purple Gallinule	Porphyrio porphyrio
Common Gallinule	Porphyrio martinica
Greater Yellowlegs	Tringa melanoleuca
Lesser Yellowlegs	Tringa flavipes
Great Blue Heron	Ardea herodias
Great Egret	Ardea alba
Green Heron	Butorides virescens
Louisiana or Tricolored Heron	Egretta tricolor
Black-crowned Night Heron	Nycticorax nycticorax
Yellow-crowned Night-Heron	Nyctanassa violacea
Roseate Spoonbill	Platalea ajaja
American Avocet	Recurvirostra americana
Black-necked Stilt	Himantopus mexicanus
Pied-billed Grebe	Podilymbus podiceps

American Bittern	*Botaurus lentiginosus*
Least Bittern	*Ixobrychus exilis*
Little Blue Heron	*Egretta caerulea*
White Ibis	*Eudocimus albus*
Wood Stork	*Mycteria Americana*
Northern Harrier	*Circus cyaneus*
Yellow-billed Cuckoo	*Coccyzus americanus*
Acadian Flycatcher	*Empidonax virescens*
Yellow-throated Vireo	*Vireo flavifrons*
Prothonotary Warbler	*Protonotaria citrea*
Painted Bunting	*Passerina ciris*

Mammals

White-tailed Deer	*Odocoileus virginianus*
Nutria	*Myocastor coypus*
Feral Hogs	*Sus scrofa*

Reptiles and Amphibians

| American Alligator | *Alligator missisippiensis* |
| Alligator Snapping Turtle | *Macrochelys temminckii* |

Fish

| Alligator Gar | *Atractosteus spatula* |

Plant Communities
Fresh Marsh
Intermediate Marsh
Submergent Vascular Vegetation
Bottomland Hardwoods
Cypress/Tupelo Swamp

Appendix I. Budget Requests

The Service Asset Management Maintenance System (SAMMS) is a system that has been used to track the needs for new projects and positions on national wildlife refuges. For this situation and the Southeast Louisiana National Wildlife Refuge Complex, SAMMS does not reflect all the present needs of the station. Since 2006, the refuge complex staff and organization has changed. Mandalay and Bayou Teche National Wildlife Refuges have become part of the Southeast Louisiana National Wildlife Refuge Complex. Below are SAMMS projects and additional personnel needs to implement the Comprehensive Conservation Plan for these two refuges.

Mandalay National Wildlife Refuge – Service Asset Management Maintenance System (SAMMS) project list

Project Name	Amount
Replace failed water control structure on Ridge Canal - Mandalay	$250,000
Rehabilitate Nature Trail - Mandalay	$30,000
TOTAL	**$280,000**

The Refuge Operating Needs System (RONS) is a system that has been used in the past to track the needs for new projects and positions on national wildlife refuges. RONS is generally being phased out by SAMMS. For this situation and the Southeast Louisiana National Wildlife Refuge Complex, RONS does not reflect all the present needs of the Mandalay and Bayou Teche National Wildlife Refuges. The RONS projects listed below represent shared funding and staffing of both refuges, as both are administered with the same budget and staff.

Mandalay and Bayou Teche National Wildlife Refuges – Refuge Operating Needs System (RONS) project list.

Project Name	Amount
Refuge Operations Specialist – Bayou Teche NWR	$90,000 (reoccurring)
Monitor Wildlife Populations and Habitat (Biological Technician)	$50,000 (reoccurring)
Control Invasive Species (plants and wildlife)	$65,000
Provide Public Outreach and Resource Protection (LE Officer)	$90,000 (reoccurring)
Restore Wetland Habitats for Wildlife	$1,500,000

Project Name	Amount
T and E Species Protection, Develop and Implement Management Strategy for LA Black Bears	$347,000
Provide Access Points and Maintain Facilities (Maintenance Worker)	$65,000
Provide Environmental Education/Interpretation Program (Outreach Specialist – Park Ranger)	$70,000
TOTAL	**$2,277,000**

Appendix J. List of Preparers

PLANNING TEAM

Kenneth Litzenberger, Refuge Project Leader, U.S. Fish and Wildlife Service, Southeast Louisiana National Wildlife Refuge Complex - Editor, Provided overall guidance and oversight

Paul Yakupzack, Refuge Manager, U.S. Fish and Wildlife Service, Southeast Louisiana National Wildlife Refuge Complex - Overall guidance, Writer, and Editor

Charlotte Parker, Natural Resource Planner, U.S. Fish and Wildlife Service, Southeast Louisiana National Wildlife Refuge Complex - Former Planning Team Leader, Writer and Editor

Pondexter Dixson, Deputy Project Leader, U.S. Fish and Wildlife Service, Southeast Louisiana National Wildlife Refuge Complex - Editor

Diane Barth, Park Ranger, U.S. Fish and Wildlife Service, Southeast Louisiana National Wildlife Refuge Complex - Editor

Barret Fortier, Wildlife Biologist, U.S. Fish and Wildlife Service, Southeast Louisiana National Wildlife Refuge Complex - Planning Team Leader, Writer, and Editor

CONTRIBUTORS

Pre-planning for this CCP began in 2006, when biological and public use reviews were held, followed by several workshops attended by stakeholders interested in the management of both Mandalay and Bayou Teche National Wildlife Refuges. Recommendations from these meetings were used during the development of this CCP. Contributors include:

Tim Ruth	LDWF - Inland Fisheries Division-Biologist
Richard DeMay	Barataria Terrebonne National Estuary Program
Paul Yakupzack	FWS - Southeast Louisiana NWR Complex - Refuge Manager
Mike Carloss	LDWF - Coastal and Nongame Resources Division
Kevin Roy	FWS - Ecological Services, Biologist, Lafayette, LA
Ken Litzenberger	FWS - Southeast Louisiana NWR Complex - Project Leader
Jimmy Ernst	LDWF - Opelousas District Office - Biologist
Janet Ertel	FWS - Biologist
James Harris	FWS - Southeast Louisiana NWR Complex - Supervisory Biologist
Darin Lee	LDNR - Coastal Scientist
Charlotte Parker	FWS - Southeast Louisiana NWR Complex - Biologist/Planner
Bob Strader	FWS - Migratory Birds - Supervisory Biologist
Barry Wilson	FWS - Gulf Coast Joint Venture Coordinator
Barret Fortier	FWS - Southeast Louisiana NWR Complex - Wildlife Biologist
Gary Tucker	FWS - Visitor Services and Outreach - Region 4
Byron Fortier	FWS - Southeast Louisiana NWR Complex - Supervisory Park Ranger
Diane Barth	FWS - Southeast Louisiana NWR Complex - Park Ranger
Robert Greco	FWS - Ecological Services - Cartographer, Lafayette, LA

Appendix K. Consultation and Coordination

OVERVIEW

This chapter summarizes the consultation and coordination that occurred in the processes of identifying the issues, alternatives, and proposed alternative, which were presented in the Draft CCP/EA; during the period of time while the Draft CCP/EA was being prepared and distributed; and during the period of public review and comment on the Draft CCP/EA.

Several teams and advisory groups were involved in the planning process with representation from the Service, Louisiana Department of Wildlife and Fisheries, The Nature Conservancy, and others as listed below.

Biological Review - October 31, 2006

A biological review was conducted for Mandalay National Wildlife Refuge by a team of 14 biologists and refuge managers representing the Louisiana Department of Wildlife and Fisheries, Louisiana Department of Natural Resources, the Barataria Terrebonne National Estuary Program, and the Fish and Wildlife Service.

Tim Ruth	LDWF - Inland Fisheries Division
Richard DeMay	Barataria Terrebonne National Estuary Program
Paul Yakupzack	FWS - Southeast Louisiana NWR Complex - Refuge Manager
Mike Carloss	LDWF - Coastal and Nongame Operations Division
Kevin Roy	FWS - Ecological Services, Lafayette, LA - Biologist
Ken Litzenberger	FWS - Southeast Louisiana NWR Complex - Project Leader
Jimmy Ernst	LDWF - Wildlife Division, Opelousas
Janet Ertel	FWS - Biologist
James Harris	FWS - Southeast Louisiana NWR Complex - Biologist
Darin Lee	LDNR - Coastal Scientist
Charlotte Parker	FWS - Southeast Louisiana NWR Complex - Planner/biologist
Bob Strader	FWS - Migratory Birds - Biologist
Barry Wilson	FWS - Gulf Coast Joint Venture Coordinator
Barret Fortier	FWS - Southeast Louisiana NWR Complex - Biologist

A public use review advisory team met in November 2006, to provide guidance for managing the education and visitor services program. Attendees included:

Garry Tucker	Visitor Services and Outreach - Regional Office
Diane Barth	Southeast Louisiana NWR Complex
Byron Fortier	Southeast Louisiana NWR Complex
Charlotte Parker	Southeast Louisiana NWR Complex

CORE PLANNING TEAM MEMBERS

The core planning team consisted of refuge staff from Southeast Louisiana NWR Complex. This team was the primary decision-making team for this CCP. This group was tasked with defining and refining the vision; identifying, reviewing, and filtering the issues; defining goals; developing objectives and strategies; developing feasible alternatives, and outlining a realistic plan for the future.

The entire staff of the complex was invited to provide input several times during the process. The core team members included:

- Ken Litzenberger, Project Leader, Southeast Louisiana NWR Complex
- Paul Yakupzack, Refuge Manager, Mandalay/Bayou Teche NWRs
- Charlotte Parker, former Natural Resource Planner, Southeast Louisiana NWR Complex
- Barret Fortier, Wildlife Biologist, Mandalay/Bayou Teche NWRs
- Diane Barth, Park Ranger, Southeast Louisiana NWR Complex

Appendix L. Finding of No Significant Impact

INTRODUCTION

The U.S. Fish and Wildlife Service (Service) proposes to protect and manage certain fish and wildlife resources in Terrebonne Parish, Louisiana, through the Mandalay National Wildlife Refuge (NWR). An Environmental Assessment was prepared to inform the public of the possible environmental consequences of implementing the Comprehensive Conservation Plan (CCP) for Mandalay NWR. A description of the alternatives, the rationale for selecting the preferred alternative, the environmental effects of the preferred alternative, the potential adverse effects of the action, and a declaration concerning the factors determining the significance of effects, in compliance with the National Environmental Policy Act of 1969, are outlined below. The supporting information can be found in the Environmental Assessment, included in the Draft Comprehensive Conservation Plan.

ALTERNATIVES

In developing the CCP for Mandalay NWR, the Service evaluated three alternatives, and adopted Alternative B as the CCP for guiding the direction of the Mandalay NWR for the next 15 years. The overriding concern reflected in the CCP is that wildlife conservation assumes first priority in refuge management; wildlife-dependent recreational uses will be allowed if they are compatible with wildlife conservation. Wildlife-dependent recreation uses (e.g., hunting, fishing, wildlife observation, wildlife photography, and environmental education and interpretation) will be emphasized and encouraged.

Alternative A. No Action Alternative

Alternative A represents no change from current management of the refuge. Under this alternative, no new actions would be taken to improve or enhance the refuge's current habitat, wildlife, and public use management programs. The existing programs would be continued with no changes. Species of federal responsibility, such as threatened and endangered species and migratory birds, would continue to be monitored at present levels. Additional species monitoring would occur as opportunistic events when contacts outside the refuge staff offer support. Current programs of marsh management would be maintained with no improvements or adaptations. No progressive wetland restoration projects would be implemented. All public use programs of fishing, hunting, wildlife observation, wildlife photography, and environmental education and interpretation would continue at present levels and with current facilities, but no programs or facilities would be updated or expanded.

Acquisition of lands into the refuge would occur when funding is appropriated and willing sellers offer land that is quality waterfowl habitat. Staff would consist of a manager and a biologist supporting Mandalay NWR and Bayou Teche NWR, along with supplementary support from the remainder of the Southeast Louisiana National Wildlife Refuge Complex staff when needed. The refuge headquarters would serve only as administrative offices with no enhancement of the grounds for public use and interpretation.

Alternative B. Preferred Alternative

Alternative B, the preferred alternative, is considered to be the most effective management action for meeting the purposes of the refuge. Emphasis will be on managing the natural resources of the refuge, improving and maintaining wetland habitats, monitoring targeted flora and fauna representative of the Terrebonne Basin, and providing quality public use programs and wildlife-dependent recreational activities. All species occurring on the refuge will be considered and certain targeted species will be managed for and monitored in addition to species of federal responsibility. These species will be chosen based on the criteria that they are indicators of the health of important habitat or species of concern. Information gaps in knowledge of refuge aquatic species will be addressed.

Wetland loss will be documented and, whenever possible, restored. Public use programs will be improved by offering more facilities and wildlife observation areas. Public use facilities will undergo annual reviews for maintenance needs and safety concerns. Overall public use will be monitored to determine if any negative impacts are occurring to refuge resources from overuse. Education programs will be reviewed and improved to complement current refuge management and current staffing. Archaeological resources will be surveyed.

Land acquisitions within the approved acquisition boundary will be based on importance of the habitat for target management species. The refuge headquarters will not only house small administrative offices, but offer interpretation of refuge wildlife and habitats, as well as demonstrate habitat improvements for individual landowners. The main interpretive facilities will be housed at the Southeast Louisiana National Wildlife Refuge Complex headquarters in Lacombe, Louisiana.

In general, under Alternative B, management decisions and actions will support wildlife species and habitat occurring on the refuge based on well-planned strategies and sound scientific judgment. Quality wildlife-dependent recreational uses and environmental education and interpretation programs will be offered to support and explain the natural resources of the refuge.

Implementing the preferred alternative will result in a diversity of habitats for a variety of fish and wildlife species, enhance resident wildlife populations, restore wetlands, and provide opportunities for a variety of compatible wildlife-dependent recreation, education, and interpretive activities.

Alternative C. User-Focused Management

The primary focus under Alternative C would be managing the natural resources of the refuge for maximized public use activities, including wildlife-dependent recreational activities. The majority of staff time and efforts would support public use activities including hunting, fishing, wildlife observation, wildlife photography, and environmental education and interpretation. Federal trust species and archaeological resources would be monitored as mandated, but other species targeted for management would depend on which ones the public is interested in utilizing.

All refuge programs for conservation of wildlife and habitat, such as monitoring, surveying, and managing marsh, would support species and resources of importance for public use. Emphasis would be placed more on interpreting and demonstrating these programs than actual implementation. Providing access with trails and by dredging for boat access would be maximized as well as providing public use facilities throughout the refuge.

Land acquisitions within the approved acquisition boundary would be based on importance of the habitat for public use. The refuge headquarters area would provide small administrative offices, a visitor center, and be developed for public use activities such as interpretation and outreach.

In general, under Alternative C, the focus of refuge management would be on expanding public use activities to the fullest extent possible while conducting only mandated resource protection, such as conservation of threatened and endangered species, migratory birds, and archaeological resources.

SELECTION RATIONALE

Alternative B is selected for implementation because it directs the development of programs to best achieve the purposes and goals of the refuge; emphasizes restoring wetlands and a diversity of habitats for a variety of fish and wildlife species; enhances resident wildlife populations; and provides opportunities for a variety of compatible wildlife-dependent recreation, education, and interpretive activities; collects habitat and wildlife data; and ensures long-term achievement of refuge and Service objectives. At the same time, these management actions provide balanced levels of compatible public use opportunities consistent with existing laws, Service policies, and sound biological principles. It provides the best mix of program elements to achieve desired long-term conditions.

Under this alternative, all lands under the management and direction of the refuge will be protected, maintained, and enhanced to best achieve national, ecosystem, and refuge-specific goals and objectives within anticipated funding and staffing levels. In addition, the action positively addresses significant issues and concerns expressed by the public.

ENVIRONMENTAL EFFECTS

Implementation of the Service's management action is expected to result in environmental, social, and economic effects as outlined in the CCP. Habitat management, population management, land conservation, and visitor service management activities on Mandalay NWR will result in wetland restoration, protection and enhancement of habitat for migratory birds, threatened and endangered species and other wildlife and fish species, and enhanced public use. These effects are detailed as follows:

- Maintain and enhance current migratory bird habitat. Enhance and restore freshwater marsh units for use by wintering waterfowl species and forested habitat for neotropical migratory songbirds.

- Maintain current resident wildlife and fish habitat and enhance these areas when possible.

- Seek funding opportunities for wetland restoration and enhancement projects in cooperation with local community groups, federal and state agencies, universities, and non-governmental organizations.

- Install information panels where and when applicable, complete and maintain the nature trail boardwalk, maintain current hiking trails, and continue to participate in community activities and festivals.

POTENTIAL ADVERSE EFFECTS AND MITIGATION MEASURES

Wildlife Disturbance

Disturbance to wildlife at some level is an unavoidable consequence of any public use program, regardless of the activity involved. Obviously, some activities innately have the potential to be more disturbing than others. The management actions to be implemented have been carefully planned to avoid unacceptable levels of impact.

As currently proposed, the known and anticipated levels of disturbance of the management action are considered minimal and well within the tolerance level of known wildlife species and populations present in the area. Implementation of the public use program will take place through carefully controlled time and space zoning, establishment of protection zones around key sites, closures of all-terrain vehicle trails, and routing of roads and trails to avoid direct contact with sensitive areas, such as nesting bird habitat, etc. All hunting activities (season lengths, bag limits, number of hunters) will be conducted within the constraints of sound biological principles and refuge-specific regulations established to restrict illegal or non-conforming activities. Monitoring activities through wildlife inventories and assessments of public use levels and activities will be utilized, and public use programs will be adjusted as needed to limit disturbance.

User Group Conflicts

As public use levels expand across time, some conflicts between user groups may occur. Programs will be adjusted, as needed, to eliminate or minimize these problems and provide quality wildlife-dependent recreational opportunities. Experience has proven that time and space zonings, such as establishment of separate use areas, use periods, and restricting numbers of users, are effective tools in eliminating conflicts between user groups.

Effects on Adjacent Landowners

Implementation of the management action will not impact adjacent or in-holding landowners. Essential access to private property will be allowed through issuance of special use permits. Future land acquisition will occur on a willing-seller basis only, at fair market values within the approved acquisition boundary. Lands are acquired through a combination of fee title purchases and/or donations and less-than-fee title interests (e.g., conservation easements, cooperative agreements) from willing sellers. Funds for the acquisition of lands within the approved acquisition boundary will likely come from the Land and Water Conservation Fund or the Migratory Bird Conservation Act. The management action contains neither provisions nor proposals to pursue off-refuge stream bank riparian zone protection measures (e.g., fencing) other than on a volunteer/partnership basis.

LAND OWNERSHIP AND SITE DEVELOPMENT

Proposed acquisition efforts by the Service will result in changes in land and recreational use patterns, since all uses on national wildlife refuges must meet compatibility standards. Land ownership by the Service also precludes any future economic development by the private sector. Potential development of access roads, dikes, control structures, and visitor parking areas could lead to minor short-term negative impacts on plants, soil, and some wildlife species. When site development activities are proposed, each activity will be given the appropriate National Environmental Policy Act consideration during pre-construction planning. At that time, any required mitigation activities will be incorporated into the specific project to reduce the level of impacts to the human environment and to protect fish and wildlife and their habitats.

As indicated earlier, one of the direct effects of site development is increased public use; this increased use may lead to littering, noise, and vehicle traffic. While funding and personnel resources will be allocated to minimize these effects, such allocations make these resources unavailable for other programs.

The management action is not expected to have significant adverse effects on wetlands and floodplains, pursuant to Executive Orders 11990 and 11988.

Coordination

The management action has been thoroughly coordinated with all interested and/or affected parties. Parties contacted include:

All affected landowners
Congressional representatives
Governor of Louisiana
Louisiana Department of Wildlife and Fisheries
Louisiana State Historic Preservation Officer
Louisiana Department of Natural Resources
U.S. Geological Survey
Local community officials
Interested citizens
Conservation organizations

Findings

It is my determination that the management action does not constitute a major federal action significantly affecting the quality of the human environment under the meaning of Section 102(2)(c) of the National Environmental Policy Act of 1969 (as amended). As such, an environmental impact statement is not required. This determination is based on the following factors (40 C.F.R. 1508.27), as addressed in the Environmental Assessment for the Mandalay National Wildlife Refuge:

1. Both beneficial and adverse effects have been considered and this action will not have a significant effect on the human environment. (Environmental Assessment, pages 79-92).

2. The actions will not have a significant effect on public health and safety. (Environmental Assessment, page 79).

3. The project will not significantly affect any unique characteristics of the geographic area such as proximity to historical or cultural resources, wild and scenic rivers, or ecologically critical areas. (Environmental Assessment, page 80).

4. The effects on the quality of the human environment are not likely to be highly controversial. (Environmental Assessment, pages 79-92).

5. The actions do not involve highly uncertain, unique, or unknown environmental risks to the human environment. (Environmental Assessment, pages 79-92).

6. The actions will not establish a precedent for future actions with significant effects nor do they represent a decision in principle about a future consideration. (Environmental Assessment, pages 79-92).

7. There will be no cumulatively significant impacts on the environment. Cumulative impacts have been analyzed with consideration of other similar activities on adjacent lands, in past action, and in foreseeable future actions. (Environmental Assessment, page 91).

8. The actions will not significantly affect any site listed in, or eligible for listing in, the National Register of Historic Places, nor will they cause loss or destruction of significant scientific, cultural, or historic resources. (Environmental Assessment, page 80).

9. The actions are not likely to adversely affect threatened or endangered species, or their habitats. (Environmental Assessment, page 82).

10. The actions will not lead to a violation of federal, state, or local laws imposed for the protection of the environment. (Environmental Assessment, page 79).

Supporting References

Fish and Wildlife Service. 2009. Draft Comprehensive Conservation Plan and Environmental Assessment for Mandalay National Wildlife Refuge, Terrebonne Parish, LA. U.S. Department of the Interior, Fish and Wildlife Service, Southeast Region.

Document Availability

The Environmental Assessment was Section B of the Draft Comprehensive Conservation Plan for Mandalay National Wildlife Refuge and was made available in May 2009. Additional copies are available by writing: Mandalay NWR, 3599 Bayou Black Drive, Houma, LA 70360.

Sam D. Hamilton   Date
Regional Director